FELL'S OFFICIAL GUIDE
TO PRIZE CONTESTS
AND HOW TO WIN THEM

by

ALLEN GLASSER

FREDERICK FELL INC.   Publishers   NEW YORK

FOREWORD

This book has only one purpose—to help you, the reader, win prizes in creative contests calling for skillful use of words, generally in praise of some commercial product.

To that end, the author has assembled in this volume every practical aid available for the composition of prizeworthy entries in the most popular contest classifications, as specified in separate chapters covering each major category.

While this book is intended primarily to bring winning assistance to those who have had little or no success so far in their pursuit of contest prizes, even experienced followers of the contest hobby should find much of value in these pages, especially in reviewing various techniques from which new winning ideas and approaches may be derived.

Readers who are unfamiliar with contest terminology are advised to consult the Glossary at the back of this book whenever they encounter any word that may have a special meaning in this field.

Some of the entry examples presented here for your guidance came from the author's own files; others are from the "Sources of Success," fully described in Chapter 13. These latter entries were created by capable contestants who have generously allowed their winning material to be made public through media serving the needs of all prize seekers.

To such warmhearted winners, who have given so freely of their own knowledge to benefit others striving for similar awards, the author extends his profound gratitude—while hoping that every reader of this book will have good reason to share that feeling soon.

ALLEN GLASSER

Dedicated to

my most precious prizes

—my wife and children

CONTENTS

Chapter 1

CONTESTDOM — REALM OF RICH REWARDS

Contestdom is a wonderful world where ordinary people can enjoy extraordinary fortune, in events like these:

For completing a two-line jingle about a popular brand of soap, a Texas insurance man was offered his choice of $25,000 in cash or the full income from a producing oil well. He took the lump sum award.

For telling why she wanted to own a combination washing and drying machine, a Missouri housewife won her weight in gold. At the current rate of $35 an ounce, her prize amounted to a plump $50,318.

For describing what she liked about a new model car, in 25 words, a young Minnesota bride won $500 a month for life. With her normal life expectancy, that award may eventually total as much as $330,000—which would be an all-time high for any creative contest prize.

Winning Secrets to Be Revealed

In a later chapter, you'll find out more about these fortunate folks and others who have won fabulous contest prizes. Right now, you may be wondering whether such exciting events can happen to YOU as well. They can, indeed—if you learn how to apply the Secrets of Winning to be revealed in this book.

You will find here scores of entries that have actually won prizes in the most popular kinds of contests—statements, slogans, jingles, limericks, names, titles, and captions.

There is no better way to learn how to write winning entries than to study successful examples of such work—and you will find them in following chapters, arranged for ready reference to assist your efforts in current contests.

First, however, let's survey contestdom as a whole, to get an idea of its size, scope and structure, so that you can better understand how knowledgeable participation in this field may make your fondest dreams come true.

Sixty Years of Contests

In the seventh decade of the 20th Century, we can look back on more than sixty years of prize give-aways in the United States since 1900. Of course, there had been some contests—more literary than commercial—in this country before the present century began, but they were too rare to be recorded here. Even in 1900, contesting was a comparatively unknown hobby, with few followers and with awards amounting to only $15,000.

By 1910, newspaper files show that $500,000 in prizes were offered, and there were about 100,000 contest fans. Within ten years, the number of prize-seekers had grown to a million, mostly attracted by newspaper and magazine contests.

By 1930, national commercial advertisers had become convinced that prize contests offered a fertile field for promoting the sales of their products. During that decade, their ever-increasing offers of cash and merchandise brought the number of entrants to nearly twelve million, and the total value of prizes for the ten-year span soared past the hundred-million dollar mark.

The Big Awards Begin

Some outstanding contests of that period are worth special mention:

In 1933, The American Weekly awarded $1,200 a year for life to William C. Gamble of Fairfield, Conn., for his slogan, "The Nation's Reading Habit"—which was used for many years by that publication.

In 1935, the biggest prize contest ever staged until that time was conducted by Seminole Tissues. It offered $125,000 in merchandise, including 100 automobiles, for the best slogans written on Seminole wrappers. This contest attracted a total of 3,264,325 entries.

Also in 1935, Camay awarded $1,000 a year for life to Miss Helen Duncan of Chicago for her first-prize letter; and Colgate-Palmolive-Peet created a national sensation with their offer of twenty free tours of Europe for the best entries on "Why I Use and Prefer Palmolive Soap."

In the early 1940's, during World War II, most all contests diminished in size and quantity; but after the war was over, they came back in greater numbers than ever, offering fabulous prizes in profusion.

From 1945, when the war ended, right up to the time this book was written in 1963, every single year has seen scores of huge prize contests, of which the following annual examples are typical.

Some Notable Contests

1945—Pepsodent offered $30,000 for finishing a statement.

1946—Magazine Digest offered $10,000 for jokes.

1947—Borden offered $20,000 for naming a calf.

1948—Chiffon Flakes offered 30 automobiles and $45,000 in cash for a two-line jingle.

1949—Colgate offered $100,000 for finishing a statement.

1950—Kaiser-Frazer offered $50,000 for naming a new car.

1951—Lipton offered $70,000 for limerick last lines.

1952—General Mills offered $100 a month for life and $250,000 in other prizes for finishing a statement.

1953—Monarch Foods offered prizes worth $100,000 for limerick last lines.

1954—Dial Soap offered $75,000 for finishing a two-line jingle.

1955—Chevrolet offered prizes worth $330,000 for finishing a statement.

1956—American Motors offered $250,000 for naming a car body.

1957—Mercury offered prizes worth $450,000 for last lines to a jingle.

1958—Plymouth offered $500 a month for life, and 18 cars, for finishing a statement.

1959—General Foods offered $100,000 for naming cakes.

1960—Gulf Oil offered prizes worth $500,000 for finishing a statement.

1961—Lever Brothers offered <u>a million dollars in prizes</u> for for last lines to a jingle.

1962—Columbia Records offered $100,000 for finishing a statement.

1963—Proctor & Gamble offered $50,000 for naming an ad character.

Why Contests Will Continue

By now, a reliable survey has shown, at least 20,000,000 Americans enter commercial contests every year, submitting approximately 45,000,000 entries annually.

Barring any major upset to our national economy, contests will assuredly continue to offer an endless flow of lavish awards for many years to come.

There are two sound reasons for this assurance. One is past performance and the other public preference. Any business-promoting method that has proved profitable—as contests have—for more than sixty years will not be abandoned in the foreseeable future.

Premium offers and sweepstakes—which entail no effort for participation—have tried to challenge the popularity of creative contests; but they have never managed to displace them from public favor, and they never will. Why? Simply because most people <u>enjoy</u> working on a contest which involves the pleasure of creating something all their own—like a name, slogan, jingle or statement.

The Best Is Yet to Come

National manufacturers and their advertising agencies are well aware of this popular fondness for creative contests. Coupled with their long record of proved success in stimulating sales, no further reasons are needed to insure the continued sponsorship of such contests by most of the richest industries in this country.

As business booms and new products appear on the market, sales-promoting prize contests will grow in profusion and prodigality. Even the biggest offers of past years will be surpassed as sponsors vie for the fickle favor of the buying public.

Is There A Fortune in Your Future?

You can share in the fortunes to be given away in the near future by learning now, through the pages of this book, how to win prizes in coming contests in the same way that others have won major awards in past contests.

Don't be daunted by the thought that you may be competing against millions of other entrants for some desirable prizes. Remember that the vast multitude of contestants submit their entries in hit-or-miss fashion, relying solely on their own vague, random, and often poorly-expressed ideas, without the aid of any guide book such as this.

Comparatively few entrants possess the winning knowledge that will be divulged here. Once you have mastered these Techniques for Triumph, you will possess a tremendous advantage over your untrained competitors—an advantage which could lead to a fortune in your future!

Chapter 2

WINNOWING THE WINNERS

Most people who enter contests give very little thought, if any at all, to the actual treatment their work will get on the receiving end. They may devote a lot of time and effort to composing the best entries they can, then daydream about enjoying expected awards; but they have only a hazy idea of what really happens to their submission after it has been dropped in the mail box.

Is such information important to you, as a would-be winner? Indeed, it is—for a thorough understanding of this phase of contesting will help you compose, prepare, and submit your entries so that they will have a maximum chance to win.

How Contests Are Judged

If you are an average contest trier—with no inside knowledge of this popular pastime—you may think that your entry will go directly to the attention of the contest sponsor, who will examine it personally along with all others submitted, select the best ones, and announce the winners.

Such is not the case. Sponsors rarely see the entries sent to their contests. The entire operation of all major prize promotions is handled from beginning to end by professional judging agencies, hired expressly for that work by the sponsor. Their procedure is virtually the same for every big national contest.

First, all entries are picked up in mail sacks—sometimes filling several trucks—at the post office to which they were addressed. Delivered to the judging headquarters, the letters are passed through envelope-slitting machines and the contents removed by clerks whose main duty is to check them for "qualifiers"—meaning the box top, label, or wrapper required as proof that the entrant purchased the contest product.

What Happens to Rule Breakers

Entries lacking qualifiers are thrown out without further consideration. Illegible submissions meet the same fate, as do those which were postmarked after the contest's closing date.

The rest of the entries are then checked for other rule violations, such as exceeding the number of words allowed, omitting entrant's name and address, failing to include dealer's name and address (if that was called for), or writing instead of printing, as rules may specify.

When all rule breakers are discarded—and they often amount to 40 percent of the total submitted—eligible entries are turned over to a staff of preliminary readers. Their job is to eliminate obviously unfit entries—those which are senseless, incomprehensible, profane, or obscene.

At the same time, decorated entries are stripped of all embellishments or copied on plain paper, since "fancy" entries are not favored by any national contest judging agency.

Prize Winners Are Picked by Points

After this come the junior judges, who rate the remaining entries according to aptness, sincerity, originality and—in the case of jingle contests—correct rhyming. Here duplication gets in its deadly work, as thousands of entries are tossed out because they sound too much alike.

Next, the surviving entries—now greatly reduced in number— reach the senior judges, who score each one by points on such elements as relevancy, concreteness, clarity, readability, uniqueness, or other special factors required by the contest under consideration.

Finally, all graded entries are reveiwed by a tribunal of agency executives, who select the winning entries according to their point rating, from the highest to the lowest. The list of chosen winners is then relayed to the contest sponsor, who will eventually pay out the prizes in the order stipulated by his hired judges.

Exactness Is Important

Now, you may wonder, in what way can familiarity with the foregoing facts help you to win? Fully to understand that, you must consider each contest processing procedure in relation to your own composition, preparation, and submission of entries.

First, be sure that the envelope containing your entry is addressed exactly as directed in the contest ad or entry blank. Suppose the announced address appears like this:

Brown Brothers, Dept. C
P.O. Box 798
New York 46, N.Y.

Don't abbreviate "Brothers" as "Bros." Don't omit "P.O." and don't write it out as "Post Office." Make certain you have the box number correct—not 789. Don't leave out the zone number, 46. And be sure to include "Dept. C." It may seem meaningless to you; but it indicates what source prompted your entry—for example, "C" may represent the magazine Cosmopolitan—so that the sponsor can ultimately learn which ads drew the greatest response.

If your address varies in any way from the given one, you may be disqualified before your envelope is even opened. However, if the same contest uses different forms of address in various advertisements, you may safely use any one of them exactly as announced.

Hints to Heed

Having been properly addressed, your letter has passed the first hurdle. It now faces the mechanical mail opener. This is a fast-operating machine which slits envelope tops after the contents have been jogged down to the bottom. If an envelope is stuffed too tightly, part of its contents will be sliced off by the opening machine. To avoid any such damage to your entry, just be sure it is folded to allow some extra space—at least one-quarter inch—within the envelope.

Since most contests have definite closing dates, by which entries must be mailed, any submission bearing a later postmark—even of a single day—will be discarded unread. So be sure to mail your entries before the announced deadline.

Of course, entries that are so poorly written as to be unreadable cannot be considered. Type your entries if possible; or write them clearly, in ink. Never use pencil. If your handwriting is not easily understood, and you have no typewriter, you'd do well to print your entire entry as plainly as possible.

Box Tops, Blanks, and Word Limits

Now comes the essential matter of qualifiers. Almost all commercial contests require you to send "proof of purchase" with your entry—meaning the box top, label, or wrapper from the sponsor's product. When rules require any such qualifier, you <u>must</u> include it—or your entry will not have the slightest chance of getting past the first mail checker, no matter how good your work may be.

The same stringent rule applies to official entry blanks and to special contest forms. When required, they must be used. However, if the rules allow a choice between blanks or any plain paper, you needn't hesitate to employ your own stationery.

Exceeding the given word limit is another rule violation that eliminates many entries. If you are told to finish a sentence in 25 words or less, don't go over that allowance <u>by even a single word</u> or your entry will be disqualified. Count every word carefully; and, to play safe, you should consider as two words such contractions as "don't," "she's," "they've," etc. However, it is quite permissible to use <u>less</u> than the maximum number of words allowed.

In addition to your own name and address on each separate entry which you submit, some contests ask for the name and address of your dealer. If requested, such information must be given.

No Decoration Needed

When entering <u>national</u> contests, do not bother to decorate your entries or prepare them in any elaborate or fancy manner. Such presentation will prove of no benefit at all, though it will not actually cause your entry to be discarded. Any embellishment will simply be removed in the preliminary processing stages. Whatever value decoration may have in <u>local</u> contests will be discussed in a later chapter.

To sum up these negative regulations, your entry must not lack anything required by the rules if it is to remain in the running. Or, to express the same thought in a positive way, you have to obey every stated condition for eligibility. Non-conformists will get nowhere in contestdom.

Factors That Win Favor

Suppose, then, that your entry has faithfully followed all stipulations and has succeeded in passing the preliminary readers. It now proceeds to the junior judges for consideration of whatever merits it may possess.

Current judging standards are based on a point system, with a maximum percentage of points alloted to each of several factors. Junior contest judges may use a rating chart with the following typical values:

1. Aptness 25%
2. Sincerity. 25%
3. Clarity. 20%
4. Originality 30%

To make your entries rate high on these four factors, you must understand the full meaning of each term. While their significance may differ somewhat in relation to various products being described, this analysis will hold true for most statement contests (with other types to be covered elsewhere in this book).

Aptness

To be apt or appropriate, your composition must fit the specific subject. Suppose you are describing a product called "Swell

Frosting Mix." It is not enough to say that this mix makes a delicious cake topping. While that may be true, it is much too vague. You must be more definite. For example, you might say Swell Frosting Mix is so smooth and creamy that it never hardens before your cake is consumed, even if left over a few days.

Sincerity

To be sincere, your statement must be believable. Don't make wild, exaggerated claims for the product. Don't say it's better than any other brand on the market. The judges will doubt whether you've actually tested all other brands or whether you're qualified to make such a sweeping statement. Instead, you might say that Swell is the only frosting you've ever tried that pleases every member of your family, from Grandpa to Junior. That sounds earnest and reasonable. The judges can believe you; and they'll consider your entry sincere.

Clarity

To achieve clarity, the meaning of your words must be so clear that they can be easily understood at first reading. Busy judges have neither the time nor the inclination to fathom entries which are in any way difficult to comprehend. Don't employ figures of speech that are too fancy or far-fetched, like calling the frosting product "ethereal as eider down." Use simple yet distinctive language. You could say that Swell Mix makes a "fluffy" frosting rather than a "light" one. Why? Because the word "fluffy" brings a definite image to the reader's mind of a delicately creamy cake coating, while the word "light" does not create any such clear mental picture. If you understand that difference, you know what "clarity" means.

Originality

To write with originality, you must avoid the obvious. Don't submit the first expression that pops into your head. Thousands of other entrants will probably get the same idea. For example, when writing about a frosting, most people will think of it as something that covers the upper surface of a cake; and that thought will lead them to say it's "TOPS for taste." After seeing this identical phrase repeated over and over by a multitude of entrants, the word-weary judges will simply throw out all entries containing that trite expression—and who can blame them for doing so? Therefore, you must strive to say something different about a product—something that will stand out from most of the other commonplace or repetitious entries. In later chapters, you will learn exactly how originality can be achieved.

Further Factors to Be Considered

After the junior judges have eliminated all submissions that failed to score a certain number of "passing points" on the rating chart, the surviving entries go through the semi-final and final phases desribed earlier in this chapter.

Since these ultimate judgments—which decide the actual order of winners—are based on varying standards, according to the type of competition under consideration, these factors will be fully discussed in the chapters on Jingles, Slogans, Statements, and other specific contest subjects.

Chapter 3

RHYME, RHYTHM AND REASON

You need no inborn poetic talent to win commercial contests based on rhymes. Even if you have never written a single stanza before, you can learn all requirements for composing versified entries from this chapter and the ones following, covering the basic forms of popular rhyming contests.

In the wide field of true poetry, there are many variations of lyrical expression—sonnets, rondeaus, ballads, odes, and other rather complicated patterns. Commerical verse, as used in most contests, also follows definite styles of rhyming; but their nature is relatively simple and easy to understand.

Three Main Types of Contest Verse

Contest rhymes fall into three major classifications:

1. Couplets.
2. Quatrains.
3. Limericks.

All three types are generally known as "jingles"; but each has its distinctive characteristics, which you should clearly recognize and understand.

The Couplet

A couplet consists of only two lines which rhyme with each other, as in this example:

This book is what contesters need
To help their entries take the lead.

The Quatrain

A quatrain consists of four lines which, in contest usage,
may rhyme in three possible ways. In the most common version, only the second and fourth lines rhyme, thus:

Within the pages of this book
A lot of tips you'll find
To make the entries that you write
Become the winning kind.

In another form of quatrain, the second line rhymes with the
first, while the fourth line rhymes with the third, thus:

You needn't be so very wise
To snare a handsome contest prize.
You only need to take a look
At winning lessons in this book.

In the third variation of this form, the first and third lines
rhyme as do the second and fourth lines, thus:

By learning how to handle rhyme,
You'll set a winning pace.
It may be used at any time
To help you take first place.

The Limerick

A limerick is a five-line verse in which the first, second and
fifth lines rhyme with one another, while the third and fourth
lines rhyme with each other, thus:

Many contests, perhaps, you have tried;
But your entries were all cast aside.
You can help yourself win;
Here's the way to begin—
Learn the methods in Fell's Contest Guide!

All Are Jingles—Each Is Different

The same general theme has been deliberately used in all preceding examples to show you that similar ideas can easily be expressed in various forms of verse.

As previously noted, the term "jingle" is often applied indiscriminately to the couplets, quatrains, and limericks which are used in commercial contests.

While it is true that such two-line, four-line, and five-line rhymes are all jingles in a comprehensive sense, they must be considered separately in this book—for each type has a technique all its own, as will be demonstrated in following chapters dealing with these specific forms of verse.

Poetic Pointers

However, some fundamental facts about versification in general should be given now. These pointers apply to <u>all</u> rhymed stanzas, regardless of the number of lines they contain.

First, you should strive to use only <u>true rhymes.</u> For example, if you rhyme the word "date" with "mate," you would be quite correct; but if you tried to rhyme "date" with "made" you would be wrong.

Similar-sounding combinations like that are called <u>false rhymes</u> or <u>near rhymes</u>; and they should be avoided. While you may occasionally see such faults in published poems, that sort of error could cause your entry to be disqualified in a <u>contest.</u> Take care, therefore, to employ nothing but perfect rhymes.

Use a Rhyming Dictionary

Where, you may ask, may correct rhymes be found, if you can't think them up by yourself? The answer lies in a <u>rhyming</u> dictionary, which may be borrowed from any public library or purchased at any book store.

To give yourself a fair chance at winning jingle contests, you should certainly possess your own copy of a good rhyming dictionary for ready reference—since you will be com-

peting against experienced contesters who regularly use such
assistance.

You've Got to Get Rhythm

In addition to proper rhyme, your versified entries should
possess the right rhythm. This simply means that rhyming lines
should match one another in accented words or syllables.

Some people recognize correct or incorrect rhythm almost
instinctively. They seem to have an innate sense of swing, beat,
or cadence. But, whatever it may be called, this rhythmic recognition can be acquired by anyone through study of such examples as the following, in which words and syllables bearing a
stronger stress or emphasis are capitalized to show where the
accent naturally falls:

> NO one WINS by WISH-ing—
> FISH are CAUGHT by FISH-ing!

Note that this jingle has exactly the same number of syllables
in each line—six. When reading it aloud (which is a good way to
learn proper rhythm) you would normally place a heavier stress
on the first, third and fifth syllable of each line. You can plainly
perceive, then, that the second line perfectly matches the cadence
of the first line.

More Models to Follow

Of course, the number of words and syllables may vary greatly in different jingles—but, whether lines are short or long, their
matching rhythm should be clearly apparent, as shown in these
additional examples of varying lengths and styles utilized by
most contest jingles:

Four syllables per line; accent on 2 and 4—

> All PRIZ-es GO
> to THOSE who KNOW.

Four syllables per line; accent on 1 and 3 —

> LEARN by HEED-ing
> WHAT you're READ-ing.

Five syllables per line; accent on 2 and 5 —

> This FAM-ous old BRAND
> Is FIRST in the LAND.

Six syllables per line; accent on 3 and 6 —

> Once you've TEST-ed our TEA,
> It's the TOPS, you'll a-GREE.

Six syllables per line; accent on 2, 4 and 6 —

> If YOU would LEAD the REST,
> You've GOT to DO your BEST.

Seven syllables per line; accent on 1, 3, 5 and 7 —

> BOX tops, LA-bels, WRAP-pers, TOO,
> MAY be WORTH a LOT to YOU.

Eight syllables per line; accent on 2, 4, 6 and 8 —

> It's FUN to PLAY the CON-test GAME,
> That LEADS, per-HAPS, to WEALTH and FAME.

Eight syllables per line; accent on 1, 3, 5 and 7 —

> HERE's a CON-test WELL worth TRY-ing;
> GO and EN-ter . . . TIME is FLY-ing!

Nine syllables per line; accent on 3, 6 and 9 —

> You can LEARN how to WIN by your WITS;
> Just keep TRY-ing and NEV-er say "QUITS!"

In the chapters which follow, you will see how these varied patterns of rhyme and rhythm may be adapted to sing the praises of every product from Absinthe to Zweiback.

Chapter 4

HOW TO WIN COUPLET CONTESTS

Couplet contests fall into three categories:

1. Those requiring two complete rhyming lines entirely created by the entrant.

2. Those requiring the entrant to compose a second line rhyming with a single line given by the sponsor in the contest announcement.

3. Those requiring the entrant to finish the first line, containing only a starting phrase, and then to compose a second line rhyming with the first.

Several examples of each kind will be given for illustration.

Complete Couplets

Life Savers, one of America's most popular confections, once awarded prizes up to $500 each for two-line jingles describing various flavored candies. Following are typical winning entries:

> Butter Rum's a taste sensation—
> Sweetens "close-up" conversation.

> Two grand flavors, blended right;
> Butter Rum, a taste delight.

> Smooth, sweet Crysto-O-Mints are swell,
> As breath refreshers, they excel.

> For tangy flavor, breath protection,
> Wint-O-Green spells sweet perfection.

> Wint-O-Green, fresh and gay,
> Is my daily "Breath Bouquet."

For after taste, a timely hint—
Refresh yourself with Cryst-O-Mint.

The smoker's perfect "Go-Between"—
Minty, tangy Wint-O-Green.

For in-between, this smoker's hint—
Real old-fashioned Molas-O-Mint.

Adapt—and Win!

Note particularly the last three entries. The writer of the final example had read the two preceding winners when they were published earlier during the course of this weekly contest. Combining the rhyme of one with the idea of the other resulted in a winning entry for the observant contester.

This is a form of adaptation frequently encountered in successful entries. It proves the value to be derived from the study of winning entry examples, as given throughout this book for your enlightenment and application. A later chapter will reveal additional sources of previous and current winners, so that you can always keep abreast of this information—so vitally important to anyone aspiring to succeed in this highly competitive field.

Short and Sweet

Here are a few more complete couplets on a variety of products:

Bit-O-Honey is an energy quickie,
Always fresh and never sticky.

Every picture's a starry gem,
When it's labelled "M-G-M."

Mouth-watering flavor, wholesome blend,
Make Peter Paul my "confectionate" friend.

Pocket ease, drinking pleasure,
King Orange gives in double measure.

Flexible, washable, smooth and smart,
Crown Zippers star in every part.

Men agree, when beards are thickest,
Ingram's takes 'em off the quickest.

Crisco fills a housewife's need
For saving, satisfaction, speed.

Strong or weak—in this fine brew
The smooth rich flavor shines right through.

Fineline streamlines every letter,
Makes your writing look much better.

For delicious taste and no-spill protection,
Safe-T Cones are my first selection.

Add-a-line Couplets

In these contests, the sponsor supplied one full line about some product; and entrants were asked to add one rhyming line to complete the jingle.

Starting line: Almond Joy is a candy sensation . . .
Second lines:

Best bar by far in my estimation.
Nuts de luxe in delightful formation.
Each sweet twin ought to win an ovation.
Tops in taste-teasing candy temptation.

Starting line: I like Big Yank for eating right . . .
Second lines:

For pep and punch it's "dine-a-mite."
Adds nourishment to menus light.
Recaptures pep that's taken flight.
So fully packed with rich delight.
Routs midday let-down for a mite.
It won my love with my first bite.

Starting line: Albers Oats are best for me . . .
Second Lines:

> Restoring pep and energy.
> For outer glow and inner glee.
> An A-1 treat with Vitamin B.
> So much to like for little fee.

Follow the Leader

Some of these "second lines" may look quite simple; but they
are not as easy to compose as they may seem. When you are
given only a single starting line, instead of three or four lines
as in other jingle contests, there is not much of a "plot" or
theme to carry on. Yet you are expected to "follow the leader"
as best you can.

In such cases, you must try to clothe the sponsor's bare beginning with the fanciest "word-robe" you can tailor to fit the
given pattern. In the foregoing examples, most of the winners
used such devices as alliteration, contrast, inner rhyme, paraphrase, and puns. Each of these winning tricks—and many more—
will be fully explained and demonstrated in Chapter 6 on Limericks.

Phrase-finishing Couplets

Most popular among couplet contests are those presenting a
starting phrase which the entrant must continue to form a first
line and then add a second rhyming line to conclude the jingle.
In this kind of contest, entrants have the advantage of choosing
their own rhyming words, as shown in the varied examples
which follow. In each stanza, the starting phrase given by the
sponsor is separated by three dots (. . .) from the rest of the
jingle composed by entrants.

While the products mentioned in these entries are well known and
widely advertised, they will be briefly reviewed before each set of
examples, so that you may clearly perceive how their particular virtues have been cleverly emphasized by successful contestants.

Soap-praising Stanzas

Ads for Dial Soap feature its protection against perspiration odor "around the clock." Described as pleasant to use, refreshing in effect, and good for one's complexion, Dial's <u>special quality</u> is said to be its deodorizing factor. Now see how winners have stressed this advertising point by relating specific benefits gained by using Dial Soap.

I'm glad I use Dial . . . I'm a social success,
Since I learned how to bathe, as well as to dress.

I'm glad I use Dial . . . it's so DIPlomatic;
It flatters and soothes—leaves skin aromatic.

I'm glad I use Dial . . . my sales record confirms
It's the way to win friends and antagonize germs!

I'm glad I use Dial . . . for romance never grows
When a feast for the eyes is a sock at the nose.

I'm glad I use Dial . . . I use it exclusively,
Though it's hot where I labor, I sweat unobtrusively.

Lyrical Laundry Lines

Chiffon Flakes is another washing product of a different sort—not for face or bath, but for laundry and kitchen usage. According to its advertising, Chiffon is notable for its thorough yet gentle cleansing power for fabrics and dishes—combining strength and mildness to safeguard users' hands. Here's how some winning entrants brought out these advantages:

I like Chiffon . . . for laundering perfection,
While giving hands such lotion-like protection.

I like Chiffon . . . for <u>his</u> clothes and mine;
It's potent for heavy things and gentle for fine.

I like Chiffon . . . such lamb-like suds
Get mulish dirt from all my duds.

I like Chiffon . . . it's my wash friend true;
MENchanting blouses retain their hue.

I like Chiffon . . . its soft, sudsy swishes
<u>Pamper</u> my hands as they <u>Prism</u> my dishes!

In the final example, note how the word "prism" has been used with such original effect as a verb, alliterating with "pamper," to suggest the sparkling brilliance of china and glassware when completely cleaned—by Chiffon Flakes, of course!

Read 'em and Reap!

You can now see that it pays to follow the contest sponsor's own ads for his products. By using salient features from such ads as a source of ideas for your jingles, you can be sure that the Rhyme and Rhythm which you put into your lines will be based on sound Reason as well—and those are the three R's that will help you Reap Rich Rewards when trying entries in verse.

Chapter 5

HOW TO WIN QUATRAIN CONTESTS

Don't watch for the word "Quatrain" to identify a contest calling for the addition of a fourth line to three given lines. "Quatrain" is used in this book to distinguish this particular form of verse from Couplets and Limericks. While that designation is definitely correct, you will not find it used by advertisers to describe contests of this kind, which they simply call "jingles."

However, you will have no trouble in recognizing quatrain contests, no matter what they're called. They all present three lines, to which you must add a rhyming fourth line to complete the verse.

Thousands of such contests have been held, and countless more are sure to come; but the few to be examined in this chapter typify their general structure and should serve to acquaint you with their winning requirements.

Million Dollar Contest

Without question, the outstanding contest so far conducted in the four-line field was Lever Brothers' offer of One Million Dollars in prizes during the latter part of 1961, promoting their full line of cleaning products.

Heralded as "the world's biggest contest," it offered more than 20,000 separate awards, topped by 27 Pontiac automobiles, for last lines to complete this jingle (which is repeated here without punctuation, exactly as it appeared on official entry blanks):

A Million Dollar Contest and who could ask for more
A Golden Opportunity is knocking at my door
To try good Lever Products and be a winner too

. . . .

According to the rules, the last word of the fourth line, to be composed by the entrant, had to rhyme with "too." This may seem too obvious for mention; but a large number of inexperienced contesters, in such cases as this, would surely have attempted to compose lines rhyming with "door" unless clearly directed to the proper word to be rhymed.

Standards for Success

The judging standards and system of rating entries for this contest were clearly stated in the rules. Since many current jingle contests have similar criteria, you should carefully consider this excerpt from the Lever Brothers rules, which served as the basis for selection of winners:

APPROPRIATENESS (appropriate to follow the lead lines, and
    appropriate as to rhyme and meter):   Up to 35 points.
FRESHNESS (interest, creativeness, sparkle):   Up to 25 points.
CLARITY (suitable and effective use of words):   Up to 25 points.
SINCERITY (believability):   Up to 15 points.

To understand the significance of these rating standards, you must see how well they apply to a random dozen winning lines which are typical of those that proved successful in this contest.

Victors on View

New shine to hopes—new pride in home—these bonus brands imbue.

With " help" adept and hope aglow, I'm doubly well-to-do.

I cannot lose, for when I use this brand rewards ensue.

Here's one more first by Lever that again none can outdo.

With Lever aids, I've leisure time to bag a bonus coup.

I'd travel into "Easy Street" through "Lever Avenue"!

With Lever to look out for me, my outlook's bright in hue.

Saves time and cents, enriches home while prizes I pursue.

No second knock required—this chance I won't eschew!

With "Lever" on the label, results to prize ensue.

My gift, a lift in household chores—no task they can't subdue.

Awards this wife much richer life—less grime, more time, prize coup!

Why They Won

Examine these lines thoroughly. Observe exactly <u>what</u> they say and <u>how</u> they say it. Note that each last word rhymes perfectly with "too." Read the lines aloud in singsong style to grasp their cadence or meter, matching the rhythm of the third line.

Then you'll notice in what manner each winning entry, in its own particular way, possesses the qualities sought by the judges of this contest—Appropriateness, Freshness, Clarity, and Sincerity. These essential features were achieved by the winners through their skillful use of such different methods as alliteration, repetition, contrast, inner rhyme, word play, figures of speech, balanced phrases, unique approach, personalized reaction or unusual rhyming word.

Why They Lost

To understand even better why these entries won, consider a couple of Lever lines that failed to make the grade. Here's one:

What better way to "clean up" could anyone pursue?

This line has proper rhythm and correct rhyme, and also a
play on the term "clean up" with its double meaning of "washing"
and "winning money." At first glance, it may seem fairly clever
and quite appropriate. But thousands of similar—if not identical—
lines must have been submitted, since the "clean-up" idea was so
obvious for the Lever contest subject.

Therefore, all such entries completely lacked one of the major winning qualifications—Freshness—and consequently were
discarded because of duplication.

Another non-winner was:

For LEVER can work wonders—as Archimedes knew!

This is certainly an original line, which hardly could have
been duplicated by any other entrant. It also makes some sense—
provided the reader knows that the ancient Greek physicist,
Archimedes, discovered the principle of a lever's power. But
the allusion was much too erudite and far-fetched for use in this
contest; and the entry was thrown out for lack of Clarity and
Appropriateness.

You can see, then, how important it is to make your own entries rate high in the specific qualities which the rules request.
Additional ways to do so are illustrated in the following examples
from other quatrain contests.

Matching Meter

> Good grooming aids are now a must
> And COLGATE is the name to trust
> For sparkling teeth and skin and hair
> . . . .

The outstanding feature of this unfinished jingle is its perfection of meter. Not all commercial verse contests offer
jingles that are so absolutely correct in rhythm. Note that all
words in each line are naturally accented in exactly the same
way: da-DUM, da-DUM, da-DUM, da-DUM. That is, the stress

or heavier beat falls on syllables 2-4-6-8 of every line, including the one to be rhymed:

> For SPARK-ling TEETH and SKIN and HAIR

When a contest jingle is so carefully contrived, you may be sure that one of the first things the judges will look for (after correct rhyme, of course!) is proper rhythm, to match the meter of the given stanza. You will find this quality in every one of the winning lines presented here.

More Winning Ways

As you probably realize by now, it takes more than perfect rhyme and rhythm to achieve success in last-line contests— and each of these examples has that extra factor which made it a winner, as indicated by classification:

ALLITERATION

I'm spick and span, no speck they spare.

Make sense, save cents, with scents so rare.

ANALOGY

That make Eyes DANCE, win Head A STARE.

Use "Colgate Street" to reach "Charm Square."

COINED WORD

"Groomerrily" with Colgate's flair.

Unveils "glowtential" hidden there.

CONTRAST

Are prized from crib to easy chair.

Will give Plain Jane a glamour air.

DOUBLE MEANING

"It's WIFE-WINSURANCE!" men declare.

These handle "U.S. Male" with care.

INNER RHYME

Such CARE helps SNARE a solitaire.

With CARE so FAIR none can compare.

Literary Lines

Finest examples of non-commercial winners are these, from a contest conducted by Sears in Milwaukee, which offered a Chevrolet car as first prize for finishing this verse:

Wisconsin Autumn scenes today
Await you in Sears' Chevrolet;
The lakes and glens and farmlands neat
. . . .

Each winning line employed a recognizable contest device, though phrased in polished literary style:

Rest russet robed in God's retreat. (Alliteration)

Sing Earthly Anthems Richly Sweet. (Acrostic—the initial letters spell "SEARS")

Are nature's roto-color sheet. (Analogy)

Are ample cause for "Wisconceit"! (Coined word)

Unfold, enthrall, inspire, entreat. (Emphasis)

Making the Most of the Least

In the Lever contest, entrants could employ as many as fourteen syllables for their last lines. In the Sears and Colgate contests, only eight syllables were available. What can one do when no more than six syllables may be used? Plenty—as these examples from the Alcoa Wrap contest will show:

> Super-strength Alcoa Wrap,
> The strongest you can buy,
> Is helpful in so many ways
> . . . .

Unlike the other contests cited in this chapter, which required entries to rhyme with the third line, endings for this jingle were supposed to rhyme with its <u>second</u> line, accented on syllables 2-4-6, thus:

The STRONG-est YOU can BUY

In these winning lines, note how various techniques have been used to make them different and outstanding:

Foil toil—Alcoa-fy! (Inner rhyme; coined word)

Foods "cap and gown" supply. (Analogy)

Yule trims 'twill GLOW-rify. (Coined word)

For ripless wrap—drip dry. (Alliteration; inner rhyme)

For "big cheese" or "small fry." (Contrast; humor)

Bids taste-leak, waste-pique—'bye! (Double inner rhyme)

When Quality Counts

There's a lesson to learn from that final Alcoa example, which was reported to be a major prize winner. Its last word, "bye," is not an actual rhyme for "buy" in the second line, since the two words are pronounced exactly alike. Real rhymes start with different letters, ending with the same sound.

However, in this particular case, the exceptionally clever pair of rhyming words <u>within</u> the line—"taste-leak, waste-pique"—apparently carried it to victory despite identical usage of the "buy" sound. Hence, in similar jingle contests, you may consider it permissible to do likewise—but only when the <u>rest</u> of your line is good enough to compensate for repetition of the same rhyme sound in your last word.

To sum up, you can see that the number of words or syllables available for your last line is not so important. It's how you use them that counts—and the fewer allowed, the greater the challenge to your ingenuity!

Chapter 6

HOW TO WIN LIMERICK CONTESTS

Of all rhyming competitions, limerick contests are undoubt-
edly the most popular. As far back as 1908, a British newspaper
awarded a huge prize for the line finishing this limerick:

> There was a young lady of Ryde
> Whose locks were consid'rably dyed
>   The hue of her hair
>   Made everyone stare . . .
>
> "She's piebald, she'll die bald," they cried.

More than half a century later, contests based on limericks
are going stronger than ever before in their hilarious history.
However, during that time, limericks have undergone a marked
change in content, though not in form.

For Fun and Funds

The humorous limerick contest, calling for an amusing last
line, still appears occasionally in magazines or newspapers,
either for the entertainment of readers or as a circulation builder. But by far the widest usage of limericks is now made in
commercial contests, to promote the sale of various products.
They are also used in campaigns for many worthy causes, such
as safe driving, fire prevention, and charitable fund raising.
Product-praising limericks generally pay the highest prizes of
all.
    There is, of course, a considerable difference between lim-

ericks created solely for laughs and those that convey a sales or
campaign message. Both versions will be given appropriate attention here.

Because of the widespread popularity of limerick contests—
which greatly outnumber those based on couplets or quatrains—
this chapter contains more comprehensive instructions for composing limerick last lines than were accorded the other two
types. Bear in mind, though, that every winning technique described for limericks can be applied with equal success to couplet and quatrain contests, as well as to most other commercial
or even literary competitions in which light verse plays a part.

What Makes a Limerick

When starting to work on a limerick contest—whether commercial or not—you should make a careful study of the four lines
given by the sponsor. Repeat them aloud (as with all jingles) to
note which syllables are accented. Grasping the rhythm of the
first two lines is most important, since your own fifth line should
have the same beat or swing as lines 1 and 2, as well as rhyming
with them.

In nearly every limerick you encounter, you will find only two
variations in the rhythmic pattern of its first two lines. One
style places the heaviest accent on syllables 3-6-9:

> Here's an ICE cream you'll EAT with de-LIGHT,
> Starting NOW, when the SEAS-on is RIGHT.

In the other model, the stress falls on syllables 2-5-8:

> "I WON-der who's MILK-ing her NOW,"
> Said REU-ben, who FARMED out his COW.

The same sequence of heavier accents will also be found in
limericks whose lines end with extra unstressed syllables, as
shown:

> Here's a QUES-tion that PUZZ-les a BUY-er—(3-6-9)
> Will my CUR-rent bills CLIMB and HIGH-er? (3-6-9)

> A DEAL-er in OR-anges STA-ted   (2-5-8)
> "With SUN-kist I'm AL-ways e-LA-ted."   (2-5-8)

While your fifth line should preferably match the meter of the first two lines, as previously mentioned, it is permissible to mix 2-5-8 and 3-6-9 patterns, since they sound so much alike. In fact, <u>both</u> rhythmic beats appear in the starting lines of many limericks, like this:

> A KITCH-en is NO place to STAY   (2-5-8)
> On a WON-derful SUN-shiny DAY   (3-6-9)

In such cases, your own line may follow <u>either</u> pattern.

Sixteen Secrets of Success

Aside from the purely mechanical requirement of proper rhyme and rhythm, your line must possess some distinctive feature, to give it a good chance of winning. To achieve this outstanding quality, you should employ one or more of the following methods, which have proven successful in countless limerick contests.

1. ALLITERATION—using two or more words starting with the same letters:

> Here's a grand way to start the day right;
> Serve prunes to your family's delight.
> > With milk or with cream
> > They are simply supreme . . .
>
> To BRing you a BReakfast that's BRight!

> There was a young husband named Bill
> Who never could quite get his fill.
> > Cold cuts he'd demand—
> > Swift's Premium Brand . . .
>
> Finding Favor in Flavors That Thrill!

"Can I handle a car!" Alec crowed,
As he sneered at a slippery road.
    You can guess what he did—
    He went into a skid . . .

Now Alec is Sad, Sued, and Sewed.

Now's the time for some brisk Lipton Tea.
It's the Change of Pace drink, you'll agree.
    You've gulped coffee all day,
    So you're ready to say . . .

"It's Pekoe for Perk-up Piquancy!"

2. ANALOGY—adapting appropriate words from some entirely different field or subject:

Coke in family-size is ideal
To serve at a party or meal;
    So get a supply
    Of each size when you buy . . .

Be an ACE with FULL HOUSE on this DEAL.

Having tried Kayser's new "Nimble-Nee,"
I'm convinced it's the best hose for me.
    With comfort and beauty,
    It does double duty . . .

SCORES a HIT without RUNS, I can see!

If you cannot see much very far,
You shouldn't be driving a car.
    It's all for the best
    To have an eye test . . .

Sight PRESERVED, in a JAM saves a JAR!

There's no other coffee today
As good as the new Nescafe.
    Its flavor beats ground,
    Saves money per pound . . .

It's TAILORED to SUIT each gourmet.

3. COINED WORDS—creating a unique word or expression by combining, dividing, or altering ordinary words:

Of course, we all need relaxation,
But let's make it safe recreation.
    For a mishap—just one! —
    Could spoil all your fun . . .

VACAUTION's the need of our nation!

A lady in search of romance
Embarked on a liner for France.
    "I do hope," said she
    "To marry at sea . . .

"Which accounts for my NAUGHTY-GAL glance."

For fresh, home-cooked soups that are best,
Lipton Soup Mixes outdo the rest.
    A cinch to prepare—
    Taste beyond all compare . . .

It's SOUPERB—for convenience compressed.

4. COLORATION—using color words literally or figuratively, preferably with colored ink or crayon for indicated shade:

If grass cutting is getting you down,
And lawn care is making you frown,
      You need more than a toy,
      Buy yourself a Lawn Boy . . .

Keep your GREEN in the PINK 'stead of BROWN!

A smart little lady named Kay
Looks for Phillips 66 on her way.
      The stations are clean,
      The service is keen . . .

Car in PINK spares "long GREEN" and BLUE day!

A youngster once got on the sly
Explosive for Fourth of July.
      When his father found out
      What the kid was about . . .

He saw RED, then turned WHITE, and BLEW high!

      5. COMPARISON—using picturesque, striking or unusual
terms in descriptive relation to the subject:

Away the blithe pennies will roll
When cold isn't under control;
      But, give Leonard a trial,
      Its bright Master Dial . . .

Guards expense like a Scot on the dole.

There's no point in wasting your dough
On a freezer that freezes too slow.
      For freezing that's faster
      The Leonard's the master . . .

For it's cold as a North Polar floe.

6. CONTRAST—using antonyms or words of opposite meaning:

"These soap flakes are sure a delight,"
Said a clever young housewife named Wright.
   "In my washing machine
   They get clothes so clean . . .

"OLD or NEW, LOTS or FEW, come out bright."

You're a careful, sharp driver, you say?
You can use this advice anyway:
   You need not be scared,
   But be always prepared . . .

To protect your TOMORROWS TODAY!

A pretty young housewife named Poe
Found dishwashing dreary and slow,
   Till she tried Oxydol—
   Speed soap of them all . . .

(a) Just right—with suds HIGH and cost LOW!

(b) Saw suds GREAT from a LITTLE soap grow.

(c) Now her WORK is like PLAY, we all know.

7. DOUBLE MEANINGS—using words which have a secondary connotation:

To college Dad sent his son, Jack,
Paying bills every year by the stack.
   Now what can Dad show
   For spending that dough?

All he got was a lone QUARTER BACK!

There is a young fellow named Spence
Who knows what to do with five cents.
   Kraft candy he brings
   To his girl friend who sings:

"Such FRESHNESS NO BUDDY resents!"

Once you sleep on a Sealy, you'll say:
"What a mattress! It's strictly okay!"
   Neither too soft nor hard,
   With its new Comfort-Gard . . .

For the REST OF YOUR LIFE, sleep this way.

There is a new wrestler in town,
Who knows just the right time to frown.
   He grunts and he groans,
   He bites and he moans . . .

Case of WHINES and SHAM PAIN for this clown.

8. HOMONYMS—using two words in the same line that sound or look alike, but have different meanings:

All your cleaning is easy as pie
When Old Dutch is the cleanser you buy.
   It's new and it's quicker
   And safer and slicker . . .

(a) For small CHANGE, a big CHANGE in one try.

(b) Cleans all WARE with no WEAR, scent or sigh.

(c) For the SPRING in SPRING Cleaning, just try!

Calvin Keene thought the road was his own,
That his seat at the wheel was a throne.
    But his kingdom has crumbled,
    King Cal is now humbled . . .

"How I've RUED being RUDE!" hear him moan.

Mary's cakes filled her heart with distress,
Some were good—some were simply a mess.
    Then the Softasilk way
    She discovered one day . . .

"It's the FLOWER of FLOURS," she'll confess.

9. INNER RHYME—words that rhyme within your line, other than the last word:

"Evervess," cried a husband named Pete,
"Is a mixer that cannot be beat.
    You save half a dime
    On a bottle each time . . .

"There's more BOUNCE in each OUNCE—what a treat!"

Safe Oxydol washes clothes white;
Mild Camay helps keep your skin right.
    Don't take it from me—
    Use both and you'll see . . .

Suds proFUSE make their USE a delight.

Marie had a lot of ambition
For movie and stage recognition.
    But the nearest she got
    Was the hat-checking spot . . .

For she SPURNED every DURNED proposition.

A lovely young lady named Mode,
Whose sport car would burn up the road,
   Tried to make it step more
   With her foot on the floor . . .

(a) When a TURN made an URN her abode.

(b) End of SCRIPT: In a CRYPT Mode is stowed.

10. PARODY or PARAPHRASE—changing a well-known expression to fit a new subject:

There once was a motorist gay;
He was—but he isn't today!
   He got by for a while
   But he drove his last mile . . .

(a) "When the BREW of the night" blurred the way.

(b) He "went down with his SIP," so they say.

(c) He learned "a BAD TURN" doesn't pay.

American Buslines are new,
Giving fast, friendly service to you.
   Our bus fares are low,
   Wherever you go . . .

Spare the "High Cost of LEAVING" all through.

The new Simoniz method is slick,
Gives you six months' protection—but quick!
   Liquid Kleener's the clue
   That cuts work-time for you . . .

Putting "Age BEHIND Beauty"—slick trick!

11. PERSONIFICATION—attributing human or living characteristics to inanimate objects or abstract ideas:

> "Delicious!" said John to his mate,
> "It's the best soup that I ever ate!"
>   "It's Lipton's, my honey,
>   And saving you money." . . .

(a) Working gal's pantry PAL CANDIDATE.

(b) Garden tang SPRINGS TO LIFE in your plate.

> Lend a hand in the safety crusade—
> In public, at home, at your trade.
>   The lift that you give
>   Will help other folks live . . .

You'll find Courtesy LEADS THE PARADE!

12. PUNS—altering the sound, spelling or meaning of words
for humorous effect:

> There once was a dude from Hoboken
> Whose pony had not yet been broken.
>   He got on his saddle
>   And sat down a-straddle . . .

But he got the BRONC'S CHEER—quite outspoken!

> A charming homemaker named Lou
> Kept her home very tidy, it's true.
>   But her pride took a fall
>   On a rug in the hall . . .

Don't let FALL-TY housekeeping trip you!

There was a young fellow named Ferd,
Who thought he could fly like a bird.
    He built wings, the poor stiff,
    And jumped off a cliff . . .

'Twasn't (W)RIGHT—only ORVILLE absurd.

13. REPETITION—repeating the same or similar words, phrases or sounds:

A much courted lady named May
Served Rath's Black Hawk Ham every day.
    "If a girl wants a man, sir,"
    Said she, "Here's the answer . . .

"No MISS MISSES MRS. my way!"

The new Simoniz method's a breeze,
Gives six months' protection with ease.
    Liquid Kleener cuts grime
    So it saves half your time . . .

Lets VINTAGE cars VANTAGE looks seize.

This swivel-top cleaner's for me,
I get "reach-easy" cleaning, you see.
    Cleaning ceiling-to-floor
    Isn't hard any more . . .

This GOOD BUY bids "GOOD-BYE, Drudgery!"

14. TRIADS—expressing three different sales points or ideas in a trio of phrases, often combined with Inner Rhyme:

Yes, Esquire Boot Polish is best,
It will pass every shoe shining test,
    Lanolizes your shoes,
    It's the polish to use . . .

(a) Style's retained, shoes are stained, cleaned and
    dressed.

(b) Steps up glow, slows bruise woe, tops the rest.

(c) Rebuffs nick, reshines quick, retints best.

The minerals that help you feel swell
And vitamins that help keep you well
    Are in prunes that you serve
    In dishes with verve . . .

Good in taste, good in looks, good in smell.

15. TRIPLE RHYME—similar to Inner Rhyme, but using
words within the line that also rhyme with its last word:

It's delicious, it's smooth, it's a treat;
For dessert, Frostee cannot be beat.
    It's so easy to make,
    Gives your budget a break . . .

You'll DEFEAT summer HEAT with this SWEET!

"Just one of those things," muttered Lew.
"It happened to me, 'stead of you."
    But Lew shouldn't have yelped,
    For it could have been helped . . .

Had LEW asked a FEW what they KNEW.

16. TYPOGRAPHICAL TRICKS—using initials, abbreviations,
or unusual effects, such as upside-down lines:

When Elsie went out for a spin,
Her car made a deafening din.
    So she lifted the hood
    And at once understood . . .

For here's how the works were within!

"I'm terr-r-ribly fond of good tea,"
Said Sandy MacTavish MacFee.
    "It must have fine flavor
    To meet with my favor . . .

"So U C Y I U's A & P."

Driver Dan let his busy mind stray
From the wheel to a home chore that day;
    Then discovered too late
    That he must concentrate . . .

¡ʎɐʍ sᴉɥʇ dn puᴉʍ ɯᴉɥ ǝpɐɯ puᴉɯ ʇuǝsq∀

To be at your sparkling best,
Drink Coke for its pleasure and zest.
    Refreshing and bright,
    Its flavor's just right . . .

C̲ heerful O̲ ffering K̲ eenly E̲ xpressed!

The final example is an Acrostic, in which the first letters of
the four words in the last line spell the product's name, COKE.
This is a difficult trick to manage in a single limerick line; but
when well done is almost certain to win a prize. See the Sears
jingle winner in Chapter 5 for another excellent example of this
technique.

A Note About Safety Contests

Among the foregoing limericks, you will note several on the
theme of safety. These all come from contests conducted by the
National Safety Council, which offers monthly cash prizes through
the calendars it issues annually. You may order one of them
near the start of any year by sending $1.00 to: Calendar
Dept., National Safety Council, 425 Michigan Ave., Chicago 11,

Ill. By so doing, you'll help a most deserving cause—and may help yourself as well.

Testing Your Own Lines

Before submitting any last line to a limerick contest, analyze it yourself to see whether it possesses most—if not all—of these features, which are always desirable and sometimes essential:

Is your line correct in rhyme and rhythm?

Is it appropriate to the subject?

Is it clearly worded and easily understandable?

Does it praise some particular virtues of the product (in a commercial contest)?

Does it contain a different, unique idea—rather than the obvious one?

Does it conclude the story or message in the given lines in a smooth, natural and logical manner?

Does it contain one or more of the Success Secrets revealed in this chapter?

What the Sponsor Wants

As a final commentary on limericks, Harry S. Granatt once wrote wittily in the Portland Oregon Journal:

> A limerick packs laughs anatomical
> Into space that is quite economical.
>   But the good ones I've seen
>   So seldom are clean—
> And the clean ones so seldom are comical!

While that may be true of many popular limericks, all quoted here are quite clean and some are fairly funny, too. But it must be remembered that humor is not sought in most commercial contests. What such sponsors want are Sales Points and Product Benefits. You've seen how to convey those ideas in various ways. Where to find them is another matter, which will be taken up in following chapters.

Chapter 7

HOW TO WIN STATEMENT CONTESTS—IN PROSE

If limericks are the most popular form of rhyming contests, then surely statements are the most popular of all contests. The reason for this is easy to understand. Many people have no knack for writing in rhyme. While that art can be learned—as demonstrated in preceding chapters—it takes some effort to acquire skill with verse. But prose is the natural expression of everyone who can write at all.

Therefore, contests calling for prose statements have a universal appeal. An ad may proclaim: "Win a fortune! Just tell why you like Baker's Bread in 25 words or less." Reading that announcement, the average person will immediately think: "That sounds easy. I guess I'll try it."

In the United States, a nationally advertised statement contest offering ample awards will often draw millions of entries. Vast numbers of people are attracted to such an offer—not only by its huge prizes, but because that kind of contest seems so simple and easy to enter.

However, despite their popularity, statement contests are not so easy to win as they may appear—as myriads of hopeful entrants eventually discover to their disappointment.

To compose successful statements, you must first understand exactly what this sort of contest requires, then learn the methods of filling those requirements in ways that will please the judges who select the winners.

Read the Rules Carefully!

In most statement contests, the first rule will read something like this: "Complete this statement in 25 words or less: I like Brand Name Product because . . . " That means you must use only <u>one</u> sentence to finish the starting phrase. You may break it up with commas, dashes, semi-colons or other punctuation—but don't use a period until the very end of your single sentence.

Know the Product!

Before you even start to write a statement for any commercial contest, you should become thoroughly familiar with the product involved. If it is an inexpensive item, buy it, use it, observe its qualities. If the subject is something costly, like a car, refrigerator, or television set, visit a dealer for descriptive literature. Study all the ads you can find about the product—and file them for future reference. Notice what features are stressed in the manufacturer's own advertising.

After learning as much as you can about the contest product, from ads and from personal use when possible, your next step is to compile a list of appropriate words and phrases to describe the product and your reactions to it. For example, if you intend to compose entries about a breakfast food, your list might include such expressions as these:

appetizing	health-building	thrifty
delicious	inviting	vitalizing
energy-rich	nourishing	wholesome
full-flavored	savory	zestful

Some of these words you can think up yourself. Some you can borrow from the product's ads. Others you'll find in your dictionary or thesaurus by seeking synonyms or related terms.

While such word-lists are essential in preparing to compose statements (as well as other kinds of entries), they provide only the bricks with which you will build a complete structure. You still need detailed plans to guide you in developing your material from basic idea to finished form.

Twenty Techniques for Triumph

In the following models, you will see how well-chosen words are put together in different designs to achieve winning effects.

Included here is every major technique available for the successful creation of statements "in 25 words or less."

Since most of these methods were defined in Chapter 6 on limericks, their meaning need not always be given; but the examples will clearly demonstrate their use. In all cases, the sponsor's own starting phrase is separated from the entry proper by three dots (. . .), and words or letters of special significance are capitalized.

1. Acrostics

In this device, words are selected and arranged to convey an appropriate message while spelling out vertically the name of the product or sponsor with the initial letters of each line, as shown:

I read <u>Movie Guide</u> because . . .

<u>M</u> ovie Guide,
<u>O</u> ffering
<u>V</u> aried and
<u>I</u> nteresting
<u>E</u> ntertainment,

<u>G</u> ives
<u>U</u> s all the
<u>I</u> nformation we
<u>D</u> esire for full
<u>E</u> njoyment of film fare.

In a Double Acrostic, which is more difficult to construct, a <u>second</u> vertical word appears within the lines, as in this example:

I like Sunkist Oranges best because . . .

<u>S</u>	uperior to all	<u>O</u>	thers,
<u>U</u>	nequalled for	<u>R</u>	ichness,
<u>N</u>	utritious and	<u>A</u>	ppetizing,
<u>K</u>	nown for extra	<u>N</u>	ectar
<u>I</u>	n every golden	<u>G</u>	lobe,
<u>S</u>	unkist oranges	<u>E</u>	xcel
<u>T</u>	hroughout in	<u>S</u>	atisfaction.

2. Alliteration

I want to see New York's 1964 World's Fair because . . . as a Native New Yorker, I know that this Exciting, Exhilarating Exposition will Make Me More Mindful of our Marvelous Mid-60's Metropolis!

The Pepsi-Cola home carton is our family's favorite because . . . we know our P's and Q's—Plenty Quantity of Purest Quality makes the Perfect Quencher for Pleasing Quickly.

I changed to Chase and Sanborn's Coffee because... choicest coffees for Flavor, expert blending for Fragrance, dating for Freshness make it Delicious to Drink, Delightful to smell, Dependable to buy.

3. Analogy

Atomic Theme:

I like Albers Oatmeal because . . . it's the NUCLEUS of a solid breakfast, with food ELEMENTS skillfully COMPOUNDED for maximum ENERGY—a POWERFUL WEAPON against undernourishment.

Card Theme:

I would like to spend a vacation at the Deauville Hotel in Miami Beach because . . . STAYING at this KING of Gold Coast hotels, I'd find a great DEAL of ROYAL entertainment, to leave me FLUSH FULL of fun!

Political Theme:

I serve my guests Pepsi-Cola because . . . it's my CANDIDATE for the FAVORITE American drink, its PLATFORM is delicious flavor plus economy, and it WINS VOTES at all PARTIES.

For more on Analogy, see Chapter 12.

4. Balanced Benefits

This technique, not previously explained, consists of paired words and phrases—with each pair citing two equally important product virtues that benefit the user.

> I like Calox because . . . it BRIGHTENS my teeth WITHOUT BUFFING away their precious enamel— the only dentifrice that combines such SAFETY in action with such EFFECTIVENESS in results.

> I like Styl-Eez Shoes best because . . . being SURE-FITTED, they make me SURE-FOOTED—with COM-FORT that puts PEP in my STEP, and STYLE that puts PRIDE in my STRIDE!

5. Coined Words

The best place to observe current word coinage in action is Walter Winchell's column, where you can find freshly minted Winchellisms almost every day. Examples from his famous news-paper feature will appear in a later chapter on Naming Contests; but here is how a clever entrant artfully used several original coined words in a winning statement:

> Insist on Champion Spark Plugs because . . . TREKSPERTS know Champion's exclusive construc-tion plugs moisture and MUCKUMULATIONS that reduce POWERFORMANCE, sparks instant ignition, nimble EXCELERATION—triggering unsurpassed durability and PURRABILITY.

As you may perceive, these unusual creations were achieved by combining ordinary words, such as Trek Experts (treksperts); Muck Accumulations (muckumulations); Power Performance (Powerformance); Excelling Acceleration (exceleration); and Purring—meaning smooth-running—ability (purrability).

6. Coloration

This device is best adapted for subjects which lend themselves naturally to it; but may also be used for general contest topics.

I use Tintex dyes because . . . when my budget is in
the RED and faded dresses make be BLUE, Tintex
puts them in the PINK and makes life COLORFUL
again!

I use Super Suds because . . . it WHITENS without
BLUING, never REDDENS my hands, and saves
"long GREEN" by keeping sheets from YELLOWING
with age.

I like Wheaties because . . . these GOLDEN flakes
turn BLUE mornings into ROSY dawns, keep my
family's health in the PINK and our food budget out
of the RED.

I don't drink liquor because . . . alcohol may cause
a RED nose, a WHITE liver, a YELLOW streak, a
DARK BROWN breath, and a BLUE outlook.

7. Comparison

I like Albers Corn Flakes because . . . they are
crisp as a winter morning, fresh as a spring shower,
and inviting as a summer breeze—the perfect year-
round breakfast food.

I use Camay Soap because . . . I've found Camay as
gentle as cold cream, as soothing as a lotion, and
as fragrant as party perfume.

I enjoy driving a Chevrolet because . . . it starts
like a shot, runs like a rabbit, handles like a polo
pony, climbs like a mountain goat, and stops like a
pillowed fist.

8. Contrast

I want to see Seattle's Century 21 Exposition because...
born in the long-gone PAST, I want to be PRESENT at
the FUTURE to learn TODAY how life will look in
that distant TOMORROW.

I like Shurfine Coffee because . . . every cup is "TOPS" clear down to the BOTTOM.

Lighters appeal to me more than matches because... lighters are graceful, matches are awkward; lighters are modern, matches are old-fashioned; lighters are safe, matches are dangerous; lighters are clean, matches are messy.

I prefer Nectar Tea because . . . many years of expert blending form the BACKGROUND which places flavor-fresh Nectar Tea in the FOREGROUND as my favorite.

9. Double Meanings

I prefer Sunkist oranges because . . . I can STRAIN quantities of rich, vitamin-packed juice from this naturally ripened fruit with no STRAIN on our food budget.

The Pepsi-Cola Home Carton is our family's favorite because . . . we get a "BREAK" in its extra content, but never a BREAK in its extra storing container.

10. Human Interest

Entries in this category derive greater effect from the writer's personal status, condition, or circumstances than they do from clever wording.

I keep Oxydol on hand because . . . my husband, an iron worker, gets his clothes extra dirty—but I can always depend on Oxydol to clean them quicker with less effort.

I like Spry best for all baking and frying because. . . as a cook, I appreciate its easy blending—as a mother, its freshness and wholesomeness—as a housewife, its much-needed economy.

I like Camay because . . . though radium therapy cured my skin trouble, it left my skin real tender; but Camay's soft, kind lather always feels refreshing and soothing to it.

11. Matching Words

This device employs several words with the same suffix or rhyming sound, strategically placed to link various phrases for unified effect.

The features I like best about Palm Beach suits are . . . their ADAPTABILITY for all occasions, DURABILITY despite lightness, WASHABILITY if soiled—adding up to all-round SUITABILITY.

I like to trade at Crown Drug Stores because . . . courtesy GREETS me when I enter, economy MEETS me when I buy, and satisfaction TREATS me when I use their products.

I like Pique Kitchen Magic because . . . it AMPLIFIES natural food flavors, GLORIFIES commonplace dishes, INTENSIFIES taste appeal of vegetables, MINIFIES expense of good meals, and GRATIFIES every appetite.

I like new super-speed Old Dutch Cleanser because . . . it DEFEATS grease, grim and hard water scum, DELETES scratching, scraping and time-taking toil, and BEATS every cleansing aid in ease, effectiveness and economy.

12. Paraphrase or Parody

These entries are modelled after well-known expressions; or they include popular sayings, suitably altered to fit the subject.

I joined the March of Dimes because . . . you can do so much, for so many, for so little.

This car-winning entry is evidently a paraphrase of the latter part of Winston Churchill's classic tribute to the Royal Air Force: "Never in the field of human conflict was <u>so much owed by so many to so few.</u>" Incidentally, the name "March of Dimes" itself is derived from another famous title, "The March of Time."

> Parker pens make fine gifts because . . . they are First in Worth, First in Style, and First in the Choice of Recipients.

This is obviously based on the Washington eulogy: "First in war, first in peace, and first in the hearts of his countrymen."

> I switched to Salem Cigarettes because . . . after trying many other brands, I found LOVE AT FIRST LIGHT in Salem's refreshingly different taste that makes a smoke TOO GOOD TO BE THROUGH.

In this example, you can readily recognize parodies on two popular phrases: "love at first sight" and "too good to be true."

13. Personification

The first entry that follows (which won $5,000 for its composer) is an exceptionally fine example of <u>Personification</u>—in this case, attributing human features and feelings to a floor mop. The second entry (also a major prize winner) employs the same technique to humanize the writer's budget and thus emphasize one of the coffee product's benefits—its low price.

> My favorite O-Cedar product is O-Cedar Floor Mop because . . . its NOSE pokes efficiently into corners; its NECK bends OBLIGINGLY under furniture; its O-Cedarized FINGERS quickly gather dust and "witches-wool," leaving floors immaculate, shining.

I like Shurfine Coffee because . . . there is a bonus of
fine flavor in every cup and its price makes my budget
SIT UP AND SMILE !

14. Problems

Like "Human Interest" entries, Problem Statements gain
their greatest effect from the difficulty described and its solu-
tion by the product, without relying much on method of presentation.

I like Ivory Soap because . . . though I live in a soft-
coal town, Ivory enables me to keep my organdy cur-
tains and bedspreads as fresh and clean as new.

I keep Dreft on hand because . . . with two families
using one kitchen, getting through quicker is necessary; and Dreft helps because it always gets my
dishes thoroughly cleaned in less time.

15. Puns

Generally used for humorous effect, this device may be employed in commercial contests where a light touch does not
seem amiss.

I prefer coffee freshly roasted by my grocer because . . . I'd rather have my coffee properly roasted
before I use it than to have it "roasted" by my guests
after drinking it.

I like those tiny little tea leaves in Tetley because . . .
these sunburst-of-flavor leaves give consistently satisfying, lip-smacking goodness—with more PERK-UP
PER CUP and less "WAIST" per sip.

16. Related Terms

In this technique, you wield several related words to weld your
entry together.

I like Sun-sweet Prunes because . . . they are vitamin-rich—GOOD for my family; tenderized for quick-cooking—BETTER for me; and inexpensive—BEST for my pocketbook.

The new Rambler appeals to me because . . . it is HIGH in power and mileage; WIDE for comfort and convenience; and as HANDSOME in performance as appearance.

I like to shop at Rexall stores because . . . outstanding service wins my APPLAUSE, competent prescription clerks win my APPROVAL, bargain values in nationally advertised merchandise win my APPRECIATION.

I use Dr. Lyon's Tooth Powder because . . . BEHIND it are many years of reliable manufacture; IN it, proven cleansing ingredients in economical powder form; AFTER it, sweet breath and a sparkling smile.

17. Repetition

I prefer Sheffield Milk because . . . coming from the finest farms, it LEADS IN SELECTION; given ultra-modern processing, it LEADS IN PERFECTION; delivered with extra care, it LEADS IN PROTECTION.

Ground Gripper Shoes are the most comfortable because . . . they STAND OUT for perfect fit; STAND UP during long wear; STAND OFF discomfort; STAND BY with arch support; and are delightful to STAND IN.

18. Reversal

This rather difficult but effective device consists of trans-posing words in one phrase to get a reversed result in the following phrase.

I like Kellogg's Special K Cereal because . . . while low in calorie content, it's packed with vitamins and minerals that will add YEARS TO MY LIFE and LIFE TO MY YEARS.

I think it's wise to wear Safety Shoes because . . .
their positive protection helps to KEEP ME ON MY
TOES and to KEEP MY TOES ON ME!

You should try these cigars because . . . they couldn't
improve its perfect blend to PLEASE MEN MORE, so
they lowered its price to PLEASE MORE MEN.

19. Sloganized Ending

Even if a statement contains no other device or special theme,
it will be more impressive if you can make it terminate with an
attractive slogan.

I changed to Chase & Sanborn Coffee because . . . its
unfailing freshness makes it so flavorful that I can
actually use less coffee per cup than other brands—
PLEASING BOTH PURSE AND PALATE.

I prefer Jergens Lotion because . . . being extra sen-
sitive, my hands require extra protection—which I
find only in this soothing lotion that for so many years
has been my STAND-BY HAND-BUY.

I like Betty Crocker Split Pea Soup because . . . easy
in preparation, thrifty in price, and delicious in
taste, it helps me to SAVE AS I SERVE.

20. Triads

Triad construction—"three of a kind"—seems to be a magi-
cal method for winning statement contests. You will find this
fortunate formula used as the basis of many entry examples
given in this chapter, even when some other special device pre-
dominates. Probably the most effective form of Triad is built
solely upon Sales Points describing three separate advantages
of the product.

I like Redi-Meat because . . . its waste-free, meal-
flattering, flavor-fine goodness—together with its

ever-readiness, energizing nourishment and absolute purity—make it our family's daily favorite.

I like Shurfine Coffee because . . . its cheery fragrance, vigorous flavor, and undeniable thriftiness give a welcome lift to lagging spirits, simple meals and pinched budgets.

New Kix Cereal appeals to me because . . . vitalized to aid health, triple-packed to assure crispness, uniquely formed to add attraction, Kix is our morning delicacy and our all-day body builder.

Varied Combinations

Pepsi-Cola hits the spot because . . . as a quick "lift," it's TOPS to the bottle BOTTOM—first in flavor, first in zest, and first in the hearts of thirsty budgeteers. (Contrast, Parody)

I like to wear Thom McAn shoes because . . . it is the LAST word in shoemanship that puts them FIRST— and the FIRST word in craftsmanship that makes them LAST. (Contrast, Double Meaning)

I use only Cooper Razor Blades because . . . there's NO pull, NO nicks, NO scrapes with Cooper—so I KNOW it has the "EDGE" on all other razor blades. (Alliteration, Repetition, Double Meaning)

Insist on Champion Spark Plugs because . . . with just a taste of gas for SMOOTH-AS-CREAM starts that won't MILK battery life, Champions save STARTING SECONDS and SECOND STARTINGS. (Analogy, Reversal, Sloganized Ending)

I like Wish-Bone Italian Dressing because . . . today's BEST DRESSED salads WEAR IT PROUDLY—a light, ingenious COATING that brings out unrivalled full flavor, SUITING the most fastidious tastes sublimely, FITTINGLY, properly. (Analogy, Personification)

I like Royal Crown Cola because . . . it HITS the TOP
in quality—HITS the BOTTOM in cost—and what a
HIT it makes with my family for genuine enjoyment
and economy!   (Contrast, Repetition, Balanced Benefits)

Versification

See the next chapter for complete coverage of this widely
used winning technique for statement contests.

What Kind of Entries to Submit

In many of the preceding entry examples, there is some element of contrived cleverness. But a considerable number are
relatively simple, and seem to rely on plain-spoken sincerity
to tell how the contest product solved a particular problem or
personal situation. While the latter approach is not exactly a
device, it is nonetheless a distinct method of entry composition.

How can you tell whether the judges will prefer tricky techniques or simple systems of expression? The truth is, no one
can possibly know in advance precisely what kind of entries
will win in any particular case—especially in the field of statements—since different types have often won in the very same
contest.

Your best bet, therefore, is to send in as many good entries
as possible—using various methods, from the simplest to the
trickiest you can devise. Most contests permit—or even encourage—submission of multiple entries. In rare cases where only
one entry is allowed, try for unique cleverness—which appeals
to most judges, most of the time.

How to Achieve Originality

There is another big advantage in composing as many entries as you can on a given subject: The more you write,
the greater will be your chance of achieving that all-

important quality in winning entries—ORIGINALITY.

Merely copying and submitting what other entrants have created—as revealed in this book or elsewhere—will benefit nobody, since top judges of national contests are generally familiar with previous winning entries which had captured major prizes.

By all means, utilize as many of the methods presented here as you can adapt for whatever contests you enter—but never repeat the exact wording of any published entry. Instead, use these examples to stimulate your own thinking along similar lines. Start jotting down every idea about the contest product or subject that comes to mind; and your compositions will increase in originality as you continue.

Unless you get a sudden stroke of inspiration—which seldom happens to anybody—the first few entries you write on any topic will be rather commonplace, containing obvious ideas occurring to countless other entrants. But, <u>as you keep on writing</u>, you'll find your run-of-the-mill thoughts being supplanted by sparkling new notions.

It's something like turning on a garden hose. At first, only stale water will trickle out from its coils—but then, as the flow grows stronger, it gushes forth in a fresh, clear, and steady stream.

So, keep your mental tap turned on full force to produce a flood of original ideas that will sweep your entries toward success.

Chapter 8

HOW TO WIN STATEMENT CONTESTS—IN VERSE

When asked to define the difference between prose and verse, a student replied:

> "There was a young lady named Lee
> Who waded out up to her ankle . . .

"That's prose. If she'd gone a little farther, it would have been verse."

Many contestants who start to work on prose statements go a little farther and wind up with statements in verse. <u>Do such rhymed entries win the approval of most contest judges</u>? Indeed they do!—and in so many cases that a separate chapter on Rhymed Statements seems well warranted.

Jingles Attract Judges

Merely by its physical appearance, the rhymed form seems to stand out and say: "Read me—I'm different!" Its brief lines, wide margins, capital initials, and symmetrical arrangement all bid for attention.

The contest judge, wearied perhaps by a succession of dull entries couched in ordinary prose, will perk up at the sight of your novel stanza, will pause to scan it more closely—and your struggle for recognition is half won! Only <u>half</u> won, though, for your verse must be distinctive in content as well as in form, if it is to bring you a prize.

Forms to Follow

When employing verse to finish a statement in the usually required "25 words or less," you will find that a quatrain or four-line jingle generally allows enough room for you to express your ideas fully without exceeding the word limit. That's one reason why most rhymed statements are in quatrain form.

Another reason is that a great deal of popular verse—which contesters naturally tend to imitate—is written in this style, exemplified in the simple but catchy rhythm of "Mary's Lamb." The cadence of this familiar jingle is indicated by capitalized words and syllables to show natural emphasis; while the number at the end of each line tells how many heavy beats or strong accents it contains:

> MA-ry HAD a LIT-tle LAMB   (4)
> Its FLEECE was WHITE as SNOW   (3)
> And EV-ery-WHERE that MA-ry WENT   (4)
> The LAMB was SURE to GO   (3)

When following the pattern of "Mary's Lamb," you may vary the number of syllables in each line to some extent; but there should always be four strong beats (emphasized words or syllables) in the first and third lines, and three strong beats in the second and fourth lines—with the accent falling on alternate syllables. Much published light verse fits this formula, as in this stanza defining a quatrain itself.

> A quatrain is a four-line rhyme
> That's never out of place—
> It may be used at any time
> To fill an empty space.

"Mary" Often Takes a Prize

While quatrains do fill empty spaces occasionally at the bottom of magazine pages, they're even better at filling empty pockets with prize money for entrants who use them skillfully in statement contests. To acquire such skill, study these examples of rhymed four-line entries completing specific statements in the style of "Mary's Lamb":

I prefer Libby's Tomato Juice because . . .

> Never weak or watered out,
> But always rich and ripe;
> Delicious, clear, and healthful, too—
> Pure Libby's is my type!

I like Kool-Aid because . . .

> In coolers for a camping treat,
> Refreshing when we rest,
> It makes our outdoor fun complete
> 'Cause flavor's "Berry Best!"

Yuban Coffee is best because . . .

> For flavor, freshness, fragrance fine,
> It's Yuban you should choose;
> For it's the tempting beverage
> That ends all coffee blues.

I prefer to save in a savings bank because . . .

> My money is respected there,
> No matter what amount;
> I'm treated like a millionaire,
> Though small is my account.

I like Stuhmer's Pumpernickel because . . .

> My children's tastes are often fickle,
> And hubby's hard to please;
> Yet Stuhmer's wholesome Pumpernickel
> Suits all with equal ease.

I use Fitch Shampoo because . . .

> I find that Fitch will keep my hair
> In healthiest condition—
> So lustrous, neat, attractive, too,
> And always in position.

I prefer Gold Crest Mayonnaise because . . .

> This mayonnaise deserves my thanks
> And prompts me to rejoice—
> For Gold Crest dressing always ranks
> The first in family choice.

Looking over these entries, you'll notice that in some cases the jingle's first line rhymes with its third line (as in the last stanza); but in <u>every</u> example the second and fourth lines rhyme— as they must in all jingles that follow the general pattern of "Mary's Lamb."

"Twinkle, Twinkle" Winning Guide

There is, however, another popular form of quatrain, with a rhyme scheme used even more frequently for finishing contest statements. In this other variety of four-line verse, the first line rhymes with the second; and the third line rhymes with the fourth. It might be called the "Twinkle Star" style, after this well-known model:

> Twinkle, twinkle, little star,
> How I wonder what you are,
> Up above the world so high,
> Like a diamond in the sky.

In each line of this memorable little poem, the accent falls naturally on words or syllables in 1-3-5-7 order. But, if you were to change the beginning of each line only slightly, its rhythmic beat would fall just as naturally into 2-4-6-8 order, like this:

> Oh, TWIN-kle, TWIN-kle, LIT-tle STAR,
> You MAKE me WON-der WHAT you ARE,
> A-WAY a-BOVE the WORLD so HIGH,
> You're LIKE a DIA-mond IN the SKY.

In its original meter, or with this minor variation in rhythm, the "Twinkle Star" pattern may be found in countless rhymed statements, since it's the easiest form of verse to compose. Why? Because this model actually consists of two couplets, if you consider the first two lines and the second two lines as separate pairs—and a couplet is the simplest basic rhyming form. Here are several examples on typical commercial topics in "Twinkle Star" style:

I like Boscul Coffee because . . .

> Fragrant Boscul, steaming hot,
> Glorifies the coffee pot,
> Adding zest to every meal
> With its appetite appeal.

I like Spry best for all baking and frying because . . .

> Now hasty baking is no trick,
> For Spry blends easy, sure and quick;
> Gives smokeless frying, free from waste,
> And leaves no greasy after-taste.

I like the 6-bottle carton of Pepsi-Cola because . . .

> Built to last for safety first,
> Snug-held contents banish thirst;
> Stores away and handles well,
> Thrifty price makes savings swell.

I like Woodbury's Soap best for my skin because . . .

To tell the simple, honest truth,
It helps retain the bloom of youth,
Which would have vanished, I'm afraid,
Except for Woodbury's fine aid.

Campbell Tomato Juice is best because . . .

First in color, first in taste,
Garden goodness without waste,
Great for drinking, soups or stews—
This red-white can bans budget blues.

I like the Eversharp-Schick Injector best because . . .

For shaving comfort, speed and ease,
The Schick Injector sure does please;
With no loose parts to go astray,
It saves me bother every day.

I wear Goodall Palm Beach suits because . . .

Palm Beach suits are "good all" ways,
Cool and smart for summer days;
Quickly cleaned and low priced, too—
Despite long wear, they look like new.

I prefer Sperry Pancake Flour because . . .

With cost so low and value high,
For better breakfasts I rely
On Sperry's special finer flour
For pancake treats my kids devour!

By following either the "Twinkle Star" or "Mary's Lamb" pattern, you can finish any statement in creditable verse. Remember, though, that composing your entry in jingle form—no matter how perfect its rhyme and rhythm—will not automatically make it a winner in a commercial contest. Your versified statement must still contain sound sales points, describing specific advantages of the product or benefits derived from its use.

Adding Sparkle to Your Stanzas

Most of the techniques demonstrated in Chapters 6 and 7 for creating limerick last lines and prose entries can be applied to statements in verse, like this one using Color Words and Inner Rhyme:

I like Shinola White Cleaner because . . .

> When dingy SHOES give me the BLUES,
> And budget's near the RED,
> Shinola WHITE makes shoes look RIGHT
> And saves "long GREEN" instead.

Parody and Double Meaning are effectively employed to complete this statement: I like Shurfine Shortening because . . .

> Home, home, by the RANGE,
> Where I gave Shurfine Shortening a test,
> There never is heard a dissatsfied word—
> For it proved undeniably best!

A clever Pun on "a la carte" helped this jingle win a statement contest about Pepsi-Cola's six-bottle carton:

> It's easy to buy a big supply;
> Our budget we're outsmartin'—
> Thrift and thirst we satisfy
> With Pepsi "a la carton"!

Contrast was twice brought into play to tell why this entrant likes Iced Tea:

> When the temperature's HIGH
> And my energy's LOW,
> A glass of Iced Tea
> Makes my "STOP" turn to "GO"!

Related Words and Homonyms are exemplified in this entry
on "Why we should all support the March of Dimes":

> By ADDING our MITE to this parade,
> We MULTIPLY the MIGHT of medical aid,
> DIVIDE the costs that must be paid,
> SUBTRACT the sacrifices made.

Analogy is used in this jingle, finishing the statement: I like
Baby Ruth Candy because . . .

> When lagging pep has me AT SEA
> And I don't feel like action,
> Rich Baby Ruth restores me with
> A RAFT of satisfaction.

An Acrostic in rhyme is somewhat harder to compose within
the 25-word limit; but here are two well-done examples:

I enjoy Grit Magazine because . . .

> <u>G</u> ood, clean stories make a hit—
> <u>R</u> estful reading—welcome wit—
> <u>I</u> nterest in every bit—
> <u>T</u> hat's why I'm so fond of GRIT!

I like Spry best for all baking and frying because . . .

> <u>S</u> ince I've used it faithfully,
> <u>P</u> a and kids have praise for me;
> <u>R</u> elishing my pies and fries,
> "<u>Y</u> our cooking's great!" they harmonize.

When Longer Letters Are Allowed

While most contest statements are limited to 25 words, some
competitions call for letters on a given topic up to 100 words.
When rules allow such leeway, the rhyme-minded contestant can
really go to town. Greater wordage naturally permits wider
range of expression, as well as a variety of poetic forms other
than the familiar quatrain.

Judges of longer letter contests seem to favor rhymed entries—probably because a lengthy prose missive may make
rather dull reading, while sprightly verse can enliven almost any
subject, as the following examples will show.

When Pillsbury invited contestants to tell, in 100 words or
less, why they liked Sno Sheen Cake Flour in a new package
with a built-in sifter, one winner used this attractive lyrical
style:

> What could be handier,
> Finer or dandier,
> Than Sno Sheen, so cleverly packed?
> Its measuring sifter
> Is such a task lifter—
> I think it's a wonder, in fact!
>
> No waste and no worry,
> No bother or flurry,
> Are known when I use this device.
> It assures proper sifting
> In one simple shifting,
> And measures are always precise.
>
> It banishes guesswork,
> Makes baking much less work,
> Without any fuss or mistakes.
> Its value is double,
> For it saves time and trouble,
> And helps me produce perfect cakes.

In another contest of unlimited wordage on "Why I Like Oakite
for Cleaning," the same poetic pattern proved successful. As in
the Sno Sheen verses, each of the following six-line stanzas uses
a rhyme scheme known as a-a-b-c-c-b. That is, lines 1 and 2
rhyme (a-a); lines 4 and 5 rhyme (c-c); and line 3 rhymes with
line 6 (b-b)— which results in a pleasing rhythmic effect.

> For cleaning my sink
> And bathroom, I think
> That Oakite cannot be matched.
> It makes them so white,
> So gleamingly bright,
> And never leaves anything scratched.

It's sure a fine friend
On which to depend,
As I've found by its regular use.
It serves me each day
In many a way
Toward keeping my home neat and spruce.

But what I like most
Is the way I can coast
Through my cleaning with Oakite's great aid.
I need no strong arm,
For it works like a charm—
All thanks to the way it is made.

No more need I scrub
To clean sink or tub;
I'm rid of that back-breaking plight.
Now it's all just a lark,
For, I'm glad to remark,
When Oakite arrives, dirt takes flight!

Effective Expression

Another excellent model to follow when writing poems for
letter contests is the Rondeau. This is a fixed form of 15 lines,
with only two different rhymes used throughout 13 lines, plus
two short unrhymed refrain lines.

While a rondeau is not easy to compose, it is especially effective for expressing one dominant idea or theme. Its rhyming
style is equally suitable for subjects in a light or serious vein,
as shown in the two following examples created by the author of
this book for contests which had called only for "letters."

The first required 100 words or less on "What I Would Do
with a Tax-free Million-Dollar Gift." Published results of this
contest revealed that some winners considered the problem quite
earnestly—but not in this case:

A Million Bucks! If I could show
A tax-free pile of that much dough,
  My frugal ways I'd put aside
  And take my family for a ride
To Florida where sunbeams glow.

I cannot say how things will go,
But I would want to have it so—
   If some kind fate would just provide
    A Million Bucks.

We'd buy an ocean-front chateau
Upon Miami Beach, you know,
   And there, in happiness and pride,
   We all would ritzily abide . . .
At least, that is, until we blow
    A Million Bucks!

A more serious note was struck by this entry in rondeau form, submitted on the subject, "Why I Want to See the New York World's Fair":

The future, fair and bright and gay,
With all its marvelous array,
   Is here revealed in imagery
    Full fashioned out of Time To Be—
Tomorrow's world on view today.

Once seen, it holds us in its sway
So that, no sooner we're away,
   Again we feel the lure to see
    The future Fair.

For here alone can we survey
A peaceful world at work and play—
   A symbol of a land that's free
   And of its brilliant destiny,
To show us all how brightly may
    The Future fare.

Acrostics Stand Out

If rondeaus seem too highly stylized for your taste in rhymed composition, and you still wish to achieve an outstanding effect with verisfied letters, you can try an acrostic poem, such as the following entry (by this author) in Walter Winchell's contest for 50 words or less on the topic, "Why I Could Never Be a Communist."

C ancelling civilized rules,
O ut to make mankind their tools;
M alicious, vicious, and vile,
M asters of menace and guile;
U ngodly, unfeeling, unjust,
N otorious breakers of trust;
I mmoral corruptors of youth,
S atanic distorters of truth;
T reacherous, cruel in creed—
S uch is the Communist breed!

On quite a different theme—"What the United States Means to Me"—
this writer won again with another rhymed acrostic.

U pon the surface of this earth
N o land can equal ours.
I t gives to every man of worth
T he chance to prove his powers—
E xcluding none by creed or birth,
D enying none its dowers.

S uch precious liberty is rare
T oday in other lands;
A nd so we find it doubly fair—
T his gift Columbia hands
E xtended for us all to share,
S o long as Freedom stands.

The two preceding examples of acrostic verse happen to be
more literary than commercial; but this form of entry is often
successful in letter contests about typical consumer products,
such as this one on "Why I Like Pepsodent Tooth Paste":

P ure and pleasing to the taste,
E ffective, safe, and free from waste,
P epsodent's my choice tooth paste.
S teady use each day and night
O f Pepsodent will keep teeth white,
D evoid of film and gleaming bright.
E xtra value for what's spent
N ever caused me discontent—
T hat's why I like Pepsodent!

Another form of rhymed acrostic is exemplified by this winner, on the subject "Why I Prefer Armstrong Quaker Rugs":

<u>Q</u> is for Quality in the name that they bear;
<u>U</u> is for Use—they are famed for long wear;
<u>A</u> is for Admirable style and design;
<u>K</u> is for Keenness in every smart line;
<u>E</u> is for Ease in keeping them clean;
<u>R</u> is for Richness that's fit for a queen.

Put them together and they will spell QUAKER—
The finest of rugs—for Armstrong's the maker!

When submitting acrostic entries—whether in prose or verse—you should make the initials which form the vertical words stand out in some way to attract attention. This can be done by underlining, separating, or enlarging the key letters, or by putting them in a different color from the rest of your entry.

Victory Via Verse

In the first part of this chapter, the quatrain style of "Mary's Lamb" was advocated as a model for short statements in verse. The same simple pattern may be used for longer letters by making each "paragraph" a four-line stanza. Here is such a winning entry by the author of this book on the theme "What 'Great Expectations' Do You Have for Your Child?"

A Scientist beloved by all,
  I'd want my son to be—
A benefactor of the world,
  To aid humanity.

Perhaps he may invent some way
  To make man's burden less;
Or find a cure that's quick and sure
  To help those in distress.

"Great Expectations," these, I know;
  But that is what I plan—
To have my boy bring world-wide joy
  By benefitting Man!

Whatever poetic pattern you prefer to use for your own entries, you may confidently expect to be well rewarded for expressing your letters and statements in rhymed form—since it
is a proven fact in this field that vivid verse can lead to victory.

Chapter 9

HOW TO WIN NAME CONTESTS

At first glance, a contest to make up a name appears to offer the easiest way to win a prize. After all, a name generally consists of only one or two words—perhaps three, at most. What could be simpler?

That's how it may seem to one who approaches a naming contest without previous experience in this field. However, in actual practice, it takes considerable skill, study and effort to compose successful entries for such competitions.

While naming contests may entail a good deal of preparatory work, there can be no question about their lavish generosity to winning entrants. On a money-per-word basis, sponsors of name contests have awarded some of the largest prizes ever paid—such as $25,000 for the single word "Majorette" as a flower name. Other awards of $20,000 and $10,000 each for one lone word have been made; while prizes of $5,000 for single names are customary in this particular kind of contest.

At this point, some distinction should be made between "Names" and "Titles" as applied to different contest categories in this book, since those terms are often used interchangeably. When appellations of not more than three words are required for any person, animal, object, product, service, symbol, or the like, they will be considered as "Names." Longer appellations—especially intended for cartoons and pictures—will be designated "Titles" or "Captions"—and will be covered in the next chapter.

Seek the Right Slant

In virtually every naming contest, the rules state that entries will be judged on the basis of Aptness and Originality.

Therefore, these two standards should be considered of paramount importance when composing your name entries.

To score high in Aptness, the names you submit must fit the specific nature of the contest subject. For example, if you were told only to name a bull, it would be quite fitting to use a word suggesting ferocity or brute strength. But, if the contest announcement described the bull as a meek, flower-sniffing specimen of the "Ferdinand" type, an entirely different slant would be required to make your entry appropriate. Aptness, then, could be achieved with wild words or mild words—depending on whether your subject was "terri-bull" or "affa-bull."

To be original, your names must not be obvious. When Bon Ami ran a contest to name its famous trademark—the newly-hatched chick that "hasn't scratched yet"—thousands of unthinking entrants took their cue from the product's own name and submitted "Bonnie." While not wholly lacking in aptness, such duplicated entries were entirely devoid of originality and had no chance whatsoever of winning.

Bon Ami's first prize—a $10,000 diamond ring symbolizing the company's 75th anniversary—was reportedly awarded for "Impecka Bill." This name was not only appropriate for both the subject (a chick) and the product (an "impeccable" cleanser) but it was outstandingly original—with a difference in conception and expression that won the judges' highest favor.

Birth of a Notion

How do you think a top prize winning name like "Impecka Bill" came into being? You can be sure it did not occur spontaneously to the Bon Ami winner. In all likelihood, this wise contestant followed a method which any name-seeking entrant can pursue with a good chance of ultimate success.

To take the first step in this name-creating system, you must compile various lists of words pertaining to all phases of the subject under consideration. Thus, if you had been working on the Bon Ami Chick-naming contest, your classified lists might look something like this:

CHICK-RELATED WORDS

shell . . . hatch . . . crack . . . coop . . . lay . . . egg . . .
hen . . . rooster . . . poultry . . . fowl . . . feathers . . .
bird . . . down . . . peck . . . cackle . . . scratch . . .
peep . . . cheep . . . barn . . . crow . . . bill . . . beak . . .
yellow . . . yolk . . . fluffy . . . chicken feed . . . paltry
sum.

PRODUCT-RELATED WORDS

safe . . . scratchless . . . sparkle . . . polish . . . soft . . .
fast . . . gentle . . . mild . . . smooth . . . clean . . .
sanitary . . . easy . . . efficient . . . speedy . . . thrifty . . .
spotless . . . flawless . . . perfect . . . faultless . . . impeccable.

Many such words can be drawn from your own mind, by the
process of thought association. If they don't come readily
enough, you can look for related terms in a dictionary or thesaurus. Searching for synonyms that way would inevitably turn
up "impeccable," which has the same meaning as "perfect" or
"faultless."

By comparing your two lists, you'll soon note that "impeccable" is a sort of chain word, linking together the sounds of
"peck" and "bill." So you break the chain apart and come up
with an exceptionally apt and original name—IMPECKA BILL—
which is probably how the Bon Ami winner did it.

Successful Naming Systems

Compiling word lists to work with is an absolute must for
for every naming contest. They provide the raw material which
you can design, refine and combine into novel creations that
will make the judges appreciate your efforts.

However, the Bon Ami demonstration is by no means the
only method for coining new names from old words. Following
are several other naming systems which have won innumer-
able prizes in the past—and can win for you if properly applied
to present and future contests.

Alliteration

Since alliteration means using the same starting sound, it is most effective in names of two or three words, such as these:

Blushing Belle   Fast Flying Flash
Java Joy   Golden Girl Gloves
Lady Littlecost   Handy Home Helper
Magic Mould   Quick Carrot Cubes
Tasty Treats   Super Speed Streamliner

However, even a single word can be alliterative if it contains syllables beginning with the same sound, as:

daydream   nearness   seaside   daffodil
fanfare   puppet   tiptop   lavaliere
mermaid   ramrod   zigzag   temptation

Analogy

Simply defined, analogy describes something in terms of something else. When the Kennedy Administration was called "The New Frontier," that was a form of analogy. So was the appellation "Sultan of Swat" for Babe Ruth and "Brown Bomber" for Joe Louis. Here are some other names of this kind, with their subjects, as used in contests:

Auto: Road Rocket   Race horse: Lightning Flash
Bicycle: Arrow Flight   Rose bush: Ember Glow
Cruise ship: Magic Carpet Train: Silver Meteor
Health food: Dynamo Power Typewriter: Hummingbird
Plane: Shooting Star   White cake: Snow Topper

Combination

More names are coined by combination than by any other single system. In its most elementary form, it is accomplished by linking two words that end or begin with the same letter, as in these examples:

Butteroyal (butter + royal)   Realemon (real + lemon)
Glamourobe (glamour + robe)   Smartog (smart + tog)

Heraldawn (herald + dawn) Reveland (revel + land)
Guardoor (guard + door) Sweetaste (sweet + taste)
Loyalad (loyal + lad) Ultrabode (ultra + abode)

A slight variation of this technique is to join words with a double-letter connection:

Bestarch (best + starch) Richarm (rich + charm)
Polisheen (polish + sheen) Youthrill (youth + thrill)

More advanced among merging methods—and more effective in winning prizes—is "Syllablending," which itself is a coined name for the process of <u>Syllable Blending</u>. These entries demonstrate how this technique works:

Beautility (beauty + utility) Orangelic (orange + angelic)
Holidaisy (holiday + daisy) Petalure (petal + allure)
Invitamin (invite + vitamin) Regallant (regal + gallant)
Medalicious (medal + delicious) Shoppertunity (shopper + opportunity)
Miraclean (miracle + clean) Ultimotor (ultimate + motor)

"Coining by joining" has been developed into a fine art by Walter Winchell. Would-be winners of naming contests should follow his column faithfully to watch him work magic with words. Here are just a few of WW's most picturesque "combinamings":

Femmedian New Yorchids
Infanticipate New Yorkitecture
Hollywoodarling Splituation
Lasstronaut Swelegant

Still another way to create a new name is to combine the first syllables or initials from words relating to the product or sponsor. Some well-known brand names coined in this manner include NABISCO from National Biscuit Company, PALCO from Pacific Lumber Company, and AMOCO from American Oil Company. In contest entries, of course, such obvious combinations should be avoided. Rather, use syllables from some apt phrase of your own composition. For example, you might name a product "PLEVAL"—explaining briefly that it was derived from "<u>PL</u>eases <u>EV</u>erybody <u>AL</u>ways."

A final variation does not actually combine words in the sense of merging or blending, but merely puts two unchanged words together to make a single descriptive term, as in these names:

Brewmaster	Fleetfoot	Newstyle
Coppercoat	Goldentart	Strongheart
Easycare	Markwell	Thriftway

Extension

In this method you add an extra syllable or two as a suffix to change a word's sound, meaning or appearance. Suffixes that may readily be used include:

ade	eer	ic	ode
all	elle	ine	ola
ama	esque	ique	oma
are	ette	ity	ona
ate	ex	ize	ore

By adding such suffixes to ordinary words, winning names like these have been composed:

Coolerama	Medality	Scarletelle
Jewelette	Nuggetine	Tropicola
Lemonique	Opalesque	Velvetex

Parody

Next to the Combination system, the technique of Parody is probably most successful in naming contests. For convenience in utilizing this method, you should compile or acquire lists of names that are famous in history, music, literature, or any well-known field. You should also possess a collection of ordinary masculine and feminine first names. Both types—notable and commonplace—may be effectively parodied so long as their original form remains recognizable.

The name of Sir Lancelot, most renowned of King Arthur's knights, has been parodied in more contests than any other famed appellation. Here are some winning versions, with the objects to which they applied:

Acrobat: Sir Bouncelot
Clown: Sir Laughsalot
Dog: Sir Pantsalot
Farmer: Sir Plantsalot
Gladiator; Sir Stanchalot

Goat: Sir Munchalot
Hypnotist: Sir Trancelot
Mule: Sir Lagsalot
Parrot: Sir Chatsalot
Pony: Sir Prancelot

You will readily recognize other famous names which have been parodied by the following entries:

Cleocatra (cat)

Dobbinhood (pony)

Eiffel Towser (French poodle)
Garden of Eatin' (restaurant)
Gay Travelero (auto)
Ghouldilocks (gorilla)

Hiawoofa (puppy)

Home Tweet Home (bird house)
Hopalong Sassily (kangaroo)
Newtopia (home)

Prints Charming (dress)
Sir Walter Roarly (lion)
Wee Huskiteers (twin babies)
Wizard of "Ahs" (chef)

Take-offs on common personal names include such entries as these:

Charlequin (pony)   Hambrose (pig)   Shortimer (dachshund)
Gemily (doll)   Pranklin (monkey)   Tabigail (kitten)

More clever examples of parody may be found in the columns of Walter Winchell, like his name for politicians who are indifferent to the danger of Communism. He calls them "Rip Van Pinkles."

Rhyme

Old Gold and Pall Mall, well-known cigaret brands, are typical of rhyming names used by many popular products. The same device has won countless prizes in naming contests, as shown by these samples:

Airy Dairy   Gay Way   Quick Stick
Clean Queen   Handy Dandy   Rest Best
Date Bait   Kill Chill   Swing King

Here, again, your lists of subject-related words should prove a fruitful source of possible rhymes. If, for example, you were trying to name a space ship or rocket, your reference list should soon suggest such rhyming names as: Space Ace, Higher Flyer, Star Car, Fission Mission, Globe Probe, Wander Yonder, and Lunar Communer.

If rhymes do not occur to you readily when going over your word lists, consult a rhyming dictionary—which should be a standard part of your contesting equipment.

Separation

This technique is the exact opposite of Combination. Instead of putting words together, you take them apart. An excellent example of Separation was given at the start of this chapter in the Bon Ami first prize winning chick name, "Impecka Bill," derived by dividing the word "impeccable."

To create names by this method, you should first make a special list of polysyllabic words relating to your subject. Then experiment with these terms until you find some which can be split into the most likely names.

To demonstrate this system once more, as was done with the Bon Ami contest, suppose you had to rename Santa Claus. Descriptive words in your list might include: altruist, amiable, benevolent, benign, bountiful, cheerful, donation, festive, generous, genial, hilarious, indulgent, jocular, jolly, jovial, liberal, mirthful, munificent and philanthropic.

Simply by splitting some of these words apart, you could devise such fitting names for Santa Claus as: Al Truist, Ben Evolent, Don Nation, Gene Nial, Hy Larious, Jo Cular, and Phil N. Thropic.

Sponsor Slant

Though most naming contests are commercially sponsored, their subjects do not always lend themselves to use of the sponsor's or product's own name in entries. However, you might try to work in some such reference whenever it seems

fitting to do so. Since many other entrants may get similar
ideas, you should attempt to apply this method in a different
and distinctive way.

This unique approach was well exemplified in a sandwich-
naming contest sponsored by Swift's canned meat, Prem. Top
prize of $1,000 was awarded for "Major Premway"—which dig-
nified the product with an impressive title that was at the same
time a clever pun on the phrase "made your Prem way." Lesser
winners in this contest also used sponsor-slanted or product-
praising names, such as Prema Donna, Premsation, and Swift
SuPREMacy.

Once in a while, though, the simplest sort of sponsor appeal
will put an entry in front. When auto-maker Henry J. Kaiser
ran a contest to find a name for his new line of cars, first prize
went for—"Henry J"!

Word Play

This final category is the broadest of all—it includes puns,
double meaning, reversal, spelling tricks, and similar devices.

A classic example of double-meaning word play in a first
prize winning name is "Gypsy Roundelayer." This entry won
$5,000 in a Gold Medal contest to name a spicy chocolate cake.
The word "gypsy" described the cake's dark allure; while
"roundelayer" not only applied to its appearance (round layer)
but suggested the recurring appeal of a gypsy melody or rounde-
lay.

"Sudsabelle" won the top award of $20,000 as a name for
Swan Soap's ad character, Mama Swan. In this specimen of
word play, the spelling of "sudsable" was changed slightly to
give that term a feminine slant fitting both subject and product.

"Seaquarium" was another first prize contest name (now
used for the far-famed marine exhibit in Miami) which could be
construed in two ways—as "see" or "sea" aquarium. In addition
to its double meaning, this name also exemplifies the art of
combination. Major winners in this field, as you will observe,
generally employ more than one minting method.

Other forms of word play have been used to coin names for
the following wide variety of subjects—some of which would fit

equally well under the Parody classification, since there is considerable overlapping in these categories.

Auto: Joyager	Mustang: Bronc's Cheer
Beverage: N-R-G	Percolator: Driplomat
Bicycle: Pumpanion	Perfume: Scentsation
Boat: Spunky Dory	Pony: Trottentot
Bungalow: Happinest	Puppy: Wagabond
Cow: Miss Americow	Race horse: Winspuration
Dog: Barkaneer	Rug: Persianality
Fishing rod: Aristocast	Space monkey: Baboom
Jaywalker: Otto Knowbetter	Space station: Blast Office
Lion: Emperoar	Speeder: Fillmore Graves
Mansion: Muchtoo Lodge	Teakettle: Mother's Whistler
Metal: My-T-Lite	Watch: Wristocrat

Summarization

To sum up the preceding advice on coining names, you
should always follow these three points:

1. Make extensive lists of words relating to the subject.
2. Consider standard names or terms in common usage that
can be changed to fit your needs.
3. Use one or more of the naming methods described in this
chapter.

Suppose you wanted to apply this summarized instruction to
a skunk-naming contest. One of the words on your descriptive
list would surely be "smell." Among your commonly-used
names you'd probably find "Melvin." Using the Combination-
Parody system, you merge those two words to form "Smelvin"—
a name that actually won first prize in just such a contest!

Chapter 10

HOW TO WIN CAPTION CONTESTS

In this chapter, the words "caption" and "title" will be used interchangeably, as they are in most contests of this general nature. Rarely is any distinction made between those two terms by judges who consider entries in this field.

Some contestants may believe that a title describes a picture, photo or cartoon; while a caption quotes what an illustrated character is saying. But, often as not, those designations may be transposed in relation to the definitions given. Therefore, you may interpret them either way, depending upon specific contest rules for proper meaning and usage.

The one thing that most caption or title contests have in common is a picture on which they are based. This may vary from a rough sketch or cartoon to an elaborate photograph in natural color. But the picture's composition is of little matter, for its entire significance to contestants is in its <u>subject</u>.

What sort of subjects are used for picture-titling contests? Sometimes they relate to the sponsor's product or service; but in other cases they have no connection at all with the sponsor's business. Both types will be fully described here for your guidance.

<u>Current Topics</u>

To foster better ways of using electricity in the home, industries represented by Edison Electric Institute sponsored a "Housepower" contest, offering $100,000 worth of prizes. It called for captions of 15 words or less for a cartoon depicting a middle-aged man and wife in this night-time bedroom scene:

Clad in pajamas, the husband is sitting on the edge of a twin bed, looking baffled and bewildered. His nightgowned wife in the other bed is watching him with mixed sympathy and disapproval. He is evidently trying to figure out where to connect a portable television set. Apparently the room has only one wall outlet, feeding triple socket plugs from which tangled wires lead to a clock, radio, percolator, electric blankets and several lamps. No outlet or extension is available for the TV set; and even if it could be connected instead of another appliance, it would drain off power from all the rest and reduce its own efficiency (as explained in advertisements and entry blanks for this contest).

That's the situation for which contestants had to find suitable captions. How did they go about it? They used the same procedure applicable to almost every kind of creative contest—making lists of appropriate words for the given subject. In this case, electrical terms like these were most fitting:

amplify	connect	generate	plug
appliance	consume	glow	power
blow out	cord	hook up	shock
bright	current	juice	short
bulb	cut off	light	socket
burn out	dynamo	line	switch
capacity	electrify	load	turn on
charge	extension	ohm	volt
circuit	fixture	outlet	watt
conduct	fuse	overload	wire

Typical Titles

From such lists, "Housepower" entrants derived key words on which they based the following captions, typifying the slant that proved most successful in this contest:

1. As Western Union says, "To avoid disappointment, WIRE ahead!"
2. CURRENT events just aren't up to date around here.
3. Don't you know that those OUTLETS are just inlets for trouble?
4. Full Housepower would eliminate this SHOCKING SWITCH-uation!

  5. Mother, can you spare a LINE?

  6. Never overestimate the POWER of your house.

  7. Remember—a SWITCH in time saves LINE!

  8. Till we're better wired, <u>turning in</u> is safer than TURN-
ING ON!

  9. WATT'S the reason we can't SWITCH to full Housepower for ELECTRIFYING results?

10. You see—over-EXTENSION always leaves insufficient
CURRENT-cy!

These entries, you will note, employ devices described in
previous chapters of this book. <u>Double meaning</u> and <u>puns</u> are
used in captions 1, 2, 4 and 9. <u>Contrast</u> and <u>similarity</u> appear
in numbers 3 and 8, while number 10 <u>combines a pun with anal-
ogy</u>.

Parody is effectively used in the other three captions, as you
will recognize. Number 5 is based on the song title, "Brother,
Can You Spare a Dime"; number 6, on the magazine slogan,
"Never underestimate the power of a woman"; and number 7,
on the proverb, "A stitch in time saves nine."

Parody Pays Off

Since parody is one of the most frequently used techniques
for composing winning picture titles, you will find great help
for such contests in collections of popular expressions, proverbs, advertising phrases and names of well-known songs, books,
movies, plays, and TV programs. Here is just a small samp-
ling of what your parody-source collections should contain:

After the ball is over	Heavens to Betsy
Age before beauty	Hit and run
All quiet on the Western Front	Home on the range
All wool and a yard wide	Home sweet home
Ambassador of good will	House that Jack built
Ask the man who owns one	How green was my valley
Better late than never	Life begins at 40
Calling all cars	Mutiny on the Bounty

Century of progress	Postman always rings twice
Charge of the Light Brigade	Roaming in the gloaming
Crime does not pay	Shot heard 'round the world
Custer's last stand	Stop, look, and listen
Desire under the elms	Straw that broke the camel's
Don't give up the ship	back
Experience is the best	Tarzan of the apes
teacher	The light that failed
For whom the bell tolls	The power and the glory
Freedom of the seas	There's good news tonight!
Good to the last drop	Trip the light fantastic
Hall of fame	Wizard of Oz
Have gun, will travel	Yankee Doodle Dandy

How such source material can be profitably used was well demonstrated by winners of the Colgate contest, which offered prizes worth $200,000 for titling a picture of a famous episode in American history. The scene to be captioned showed Benjamin Franklin flying his kite during a storm, amid heavy rain and flashes of lightning. His kite string carried a key used in his experiment to reveal the electrical nature of lightning.

Leads from Lists

Experienced entrants in this contest, after studying all details depicted, first compiled a list of electrical terms—such as the "Housepower" words given earlier in this chapter—and added other expressions with a scientific and patriotic slant, pertaining directly to the Franklin picture.

These specific word lists, considered in conjunction with general collections of familiar terms, brought forth the following winning titles, each employing the art of parody:

Amp-bassador of good skill	Power for men and glory for Ben
Charge of the kite rig aid	Squall of fame
Experiment is the best reacher	Tapping the light fantastic

Heavens to Benny!   The short seen 'round the
                                    world

Ohming in the gloaming   Yankee did all dandy

Devices other than parody which proved successful in titling
the Franklin picture included the following:

Alliteration: Riddle Resolving Rendezvous.
Analogy: Current dividend from a key investment.
Coined word: Communikiting with nature.
Color: Bolt from blue makes red letter day.
Contrast: The high sign that gave the lowdown.
Double meaning: Founding father in a shocking situation.
Homonym: A tale within a tail.
Humor: He's nuts about bolts.
Pun: And soddenly he saw the light!
Related words: A raisin' that grew into a current.
Similarity: From his wits came our watts.
Verse: Ben's bolt brings volt.

You will notice that several of these winners combined various techniques suitable for this sort of contest. For example,
the title "He's nuts about bolts" has humor, double meaning,
and related words. Caption contests allow a wide latitude of
usable devices; and you may even kid the subject—so long as it
does not refer to the sponsor's product, which of course is
sacrosanct.

Picturing the Product

Puss 'n Boots supplied a good example of a title contest based
upon a picture concerning the sponsor's product, advertised as
"America's largest-selling cat food."
Ads for this contest featured an attractive, natural-color
photograph of a mother cat and four kittens beside a grocery
shopping bag from which several cans of Puss 'n Boots have
been removed. Looking upward expectantly, the cats appeared
to await opening of the cans for their enjoyment.
Here, again, the first step was to list words appropriate
for the subject of the picture—not only for the cats shown,

but for their favorite food, Puss 'n Boots, thus:

Cat Words

cat	fur	paws	puss
claws	glossy	pet	sleek
coat	kitten	playful	tail
feline	mew	purr	whiskers

Product Words

appetite	feed	meal	nutrition
can	fish	minerals	pep
diet	growth	natural	protein
energy	health	nourishing	vitamins

These words could be derived directly from the Puss 'n Boots ads, contest blank and can label, as well as from the entrant's own mind, dictionary or thesaurus. From such sources, the following titles were composed, using indicated devices:

There's good MEWS tonight—Puss 'n Boots for cats' delight! (parody and rhyme)

Puss 'n Boots makes all cats stop, look and GLISTEN. (parody)

SLEEK operators corner the Puss 'n Boots market. (analogy)

FISHING for Puss 'n Boots with NATURAL-LURE. (coined word and analogy)

On Puss 'n Boots they solely dine—which keeps them always FELINE fine! (pun and rhyme)

Just in Jest

When sponsored by newspapers or magazines, rather than by product manufacturers, cartoon caption contests seek only

humorous gag lines. This slant was well illustrated by winners
in a contest conducted by the New York Daily News, which
awarded top prizes for these titles for the cartoons described:

> Man with bandaged nose meets friend, who observes:
> "Well, pal, I see you lost a big nasal battle."

> Fat woman on scale, with husband watching. He says:
> "What you need is mind over platter, dear."

> Woman to clerk at perfume counter: "It did drive him
> mad, but now I only see him on visiting days."

> Doctor with medical satchel is buying "Get Well" cards.
> Observer quips: "It's not in the cards, Doc—it's in the
> bag."

> Little girl, overhearing father's comment on TV ac-
> tress, asks: "Mommy, isn't an 'eyeful' a tower in
> France?"

> Offering dish-towel to reluctant husband, wife remarks:
> "It's guaranteed not to shrink from washing—why
> should you?"

Safety Sayings

Since safety is a recurrent theme in caption contests, you
can prepare for coming competitions on this subject by studying
some cartoon titles which won prizes from the National Safety
Council. Most of them, you will note, contain puns or word
play:

Cartoon:	Wife smoking in bed, as husband rushes in with fire extinguisher.
Title:	"Are you trying to make us FLAMOUS over night?"

Cartoon:	Husband is standing on shaky boxes stacked on a chair to fix a ceiling light socket, while wife watches fearfully.
Title:	"The RUNG approach would be RIGHT here!"

Cartoon: Supervisor rebuking girl worker with long loose hair-do, as she operates pressing machine.

Title: "A perfect CRIPPLE PLAY—tresses to presses to messes!"

Cartoon: Groom stumbles on loose rug while carrying bride through doorway.

Title: "Is this our TRIP to the FALLS?"

Cartoon: A woman trying to park her car is beaten to the space by a sneaky male driver.

Title: "When you CUT IN, you CUT OUT road safety!"

Cartoon: Mother slips on a child's plaything carelessly left on the floor.

Title: "The SITE of a toy UPSET her."

Quoting the Kiddies

No lesson on picture titling would be complete without covering the subject most often used—Babies. Hundreds of contests, national as well as local, have been based on photos of infants wearing all sorts of expressions—and little else.

Entrants are asked to tell what the pictured baby is supposed to be saying. Winning captions in such contests rarely contain tricky words or devices. They depend mostly on the comic effect of making the tot utter a mature, sophisticated remark that could apply only to the world of adults. Here are some winners showing this slant, based on the baby's described expression, as they appeared in another New York Daily News contest:

Tired and displeased, rubbing one eye wearily: "Well, maybe the second act will be better."

Holding rattle aloft with puzzled look: "You mean I was waving this at the office party?"

Indignant attitude: "Yeah, I told off the boss like you said—so I'm home early!"

Smiling coyly: "You must be mistaken, miss. All I whistled for was a cab!"

Frowning in concentration: "Now where did I spend that five?"

Lips twisted in a sneer: "Don't take an inventory of your purse now, lady! Just deposit your bus fare!"

Annoyed appearance: "A little service at this end of the counter, please!"

Rubbing nose disgustedly: "Oh brother, do I need a new gag writer!"

Whether you're composing a title for a simple baby picture or a scene of comparative complexity, remember this prize-winning pointer:

Study the subject till you perceive some special significance in it—then create a caption to convey that significance to the contest judges so vividly that you'll surely be "entitled" to an award.

Chapter 11

HOW TO WIN SLOGAN CONTESTS

"Today's Big Contest Winners Were Yesterday's Beginners."
That's a slogan—and a good one. It's specific, mentioning the
subject it covers—contests. It has rhythm—read it aloud and
note the swing. It has contrast—"today" and "yesterday." It has
rhyme and alliteration—"big winners" and "beginners." It employs effective figures of speech—"today" for present, "yesterday" for past. It is brief, memorable and impressive—once read,
it lingers in your mind. And it has the ring of universal truth—
for all outstanding winners, in every field of endeavor, were at
one time only beginners.

You will find some of those characteristics in most prize-
winning slogans, along with other distinctive qualities to be considered here. First, however, you should understand the nature and purpose of a slogan, as used in contests and advertising.

A slogan should say a lot in a few words. It may describe
the virtues of a product, advise a course of action, or epitomize
generally known facts—as in the phrase at the start of this chapter. But whatever its intention, it should be brief, clear, and to
the point. A whole lesson on slogan writing could be capsuled
into three words: To sloganize, summarize!

Naturally, if you want to summarize the essentials of any
subject, you must know it quite thoroughly. So the first step in
composing slogans—as with other forms of entries—is to become familiar with the contest subject from every source available. Next comes the inevitable compilation of appropriate word
lists—a preliminary advocated for all creative contests.

After collecting your basic material, select salient terms
that may be woven into striking slogans by using one or

more winning techniques to be illustrated here.

You will find these methods much like the ones recommended for creation of contest statements in Chapter 7—which is not surprising, since a slogan is actually a statement stripped of all excess verbiage, boiled down to its essence, refined and reformed into a sparkling new expression that crystallizes a keynote idea.

Successful Slogan Systems

Each slogan exemplifying one of the following techniques has its subject identified, so that you may perceive how effectively the slogan fulfills its purpose.

Many of these examples illustrate more than the single creative method under which they are classified, as indicated in parentheses after such slogans.

Acrostic

Coal: <u>C</u> omfort <u>O</u> f <u>A</u> merican <u>L</u> ife.

Fish: <u>F</u> ish <u>I</u> nsures <u>S</u> ound <u>H</u> ealth.

Alliteration

Auto: Best bet's a Buick.

Canned corn: Fresh from Flavorland.

Florida fashions: Sunny styles for sunny living. (<u>re</u>petition)

Washer: Most wanted by most women. (<u>repetition</u>)

Analogy

Cancer fund: Arrest cancer—it's wanted for murder!

Oranges: Live wires need plenty of juice.

Wallet: Snug corral for roving bucks.

Balanced Phrases

Charity: The most you can give is the least you can do. (contrast)

Classified ads: Read for profit—use for results.

Shortening: Bans smoke and smell—blends fast and well. (rhyme)

Tomato juice: A stop to thirst—a step to health. (similarity)

Coined Words

Salve: Just the thing for skinjuries.

Shoes: More styleage, more mileage, more smile-age. (rhyme, repetition, alliteration, triad)

Color Words

Department store: Make our silver anniversary your golden shopportunity. (coined word)

Laundry soap: Makes blue Monday a red letter day for washing.

Comparison

Moccasins: Like strolling on a cloud.

Soap: A soap-clean complexion with cold-cream protection. (rhyme)

Contrast

Flour: Stop making blunders—start baking wonders! (alliteration, rhyme)

Freewheeling: The coming way of going places.

Gasoline: Travel in high at low cost.

Shoes: Outer beauty, inner worth.

TV station: The first word in news—the last word in entertainment.

Double Meaning

Auto: Smart as its owner.

Peanuts: When hunger drives you nutty—eat Tom's.

Tissue: What a material difference!

Underwear: Next to myself I like B.V.D. best.

Parody

Adhesive: It's so nice to have a can around the house.

Coffee: Man's best blend.

Diapers: Rock-a-dry baby.

Doughnuts: What foods these morsels be!

Liquor: It reigns where it pours.

Masseur: The paws that refresh.

Race track: The greatest show on turf.

Shoes: For a Happy Shoe Year.

Suntan lotion: Get what you bask for.

Toothpaste: A miss is as good as her smile.

TV network: Sales through the air with the greatest of ease.

Personification

Automatic range: Unties your apron strings.

Candy: The sweetheart of a chewsy world. (pun)

Ketchup: The best pal a good meal ever had.

Magazine: Speaks the language of humanity.

Tire: The tire that laughs at flats.

Pun

Girdle: Leaves you breadth-less.

Milk: Moo power to you!

Potato chips: Merry Crisp-ness!

Stapler: Does so many fasten-ating things.

Station wagon: Tops the tote-em poll.

Water softener: America's wash-word.

Repetition

Dress: Makes women look nice and men look twice. (rhyme)

Drug store: Be safe, be sure, be thrifty—buy Rexall! (alliteration)

Noodles: For balanced meals on balanced budgets.

Reversal

Cancer fund: Check cancer with a cancer check.

Paint: Use a good finish, and finish for good.

Pen: Exactly right to write exactly.

Radio station: People listen to us because we listen to people.

Zipper: Smoothly finished to finish smoothly.

Rhyme

Apple: An apple a day keeps the doctor away.

Beverage: More bounce to the ounce.

Bus: Convenience plus—go by bus.

Carpet: Home means more with carpet on the floor.

Coffee: Toasting protects what blending perfects. (alliteration)

Magazine: Its best reference is public preference. (alliteration)

Meat: The ham what am.

Paper cup: A better cup from bottom up. (alliteration)

Pull-out tissues: No fumble—no jumble—no grumble. (triad, repetition)

Zipper: It hides as it slides.

Similarity

Coffee: There's more pick-up per cup.

Ice cream: The cheeriest, cherryest ice cream ever.

Light bulb: A good buy to see by.

Magazine: Spokesman for America's sportsmen.

Percolator: Change bitter coffee to better coffee.

Sponsor Slant

Camera: If it isn't an Eastman, it isn't a Kodak.

Cereal: If the last flake crackles—it's Kellogg's.

Frozen food: Only the finest is chosen to be frozen by Libby's.

Gasoline: Stop at Sunoco—go with confidence! (contrast)

Triad

Auto: Eye it—try it—buy it! (rhyme)

Beer: Purity, body, flavor.

Magazine: Brief, thrilling, authentic.

Razor blade: Look sharp—feel sharp—be sharp! (repetition)

Shortening: Easy to blend, easier to bake, easiest to digest. (repetition)

Vacuum cleaner: It beats, as it sweeps, as it cleans. (similarity of "ee" sound)

Washington State: It's cool, it's green, it's great! (alliteration)

Word Play

Awning: Just a shade better.

Ballpoint pen: Write on the ball.

Bra: Your bosom friend. (personification)

Lawn sprinkler: Dew it yourself.

Savings bank: A weekly habit that grows on you.

Shirt: Give your beau an Arrow. (analogy)

Typical Winning Slogans

To note how some of the foregoing methods were successfully applied in typical contests, consider first the "Slogan for Wood" competition sponsored by the National Lumber Manufacturing Association, which awarded prizes for the following entries:

First, $5,000: Certified by centuries of service. (alliteration)

Second, $2,000: Wood—use it; nature renews it. (rhyme, balanced phrase)

Other winning slogans in this contest embodied various techniques as indicated:

Build better with better lumber (<u>repetition, alliteration</u>)

For building needs, lumber leads. (<u>rhyme, alliteration</u>)

A growing supply for a growing demand. (<u>repetition, double meaning</u>)

Your judgment is good when you build with wood. (<u>rhyme</u>)

The more you use it, the better you like it. (<u>balanced phrase</u>)

Always in demand—always at hand. (<u>rhyme, repetition</u>)

Ever growing in forest and in favor. (<u>alliteration, double meaning</u>)

Wood ways are wise ways. (<u>alliteration, repetition</u>)

Wood serves, survives and satisfies. (<u>triad, alliteration</u>)

Another contest, requiring slogans for the Nationwide Trailer Rental System, brought forth these winners, exemplifying methods which should be recognizable by now:

First, $1,000:   A little pull goes a long way.

Second, $500:   The haul of fame.

Third, $100:   The greatest tow on earth.

Other prizes were awarded for these trailer slogans:

Nationwide coast to coast—costs the least, hauls the most.

So easy to become attached to us.

We lower the high cost of leaving.

Moving near, moving far—load a trailer, not your car.

Safe Driving Slogans

Of all slogan themes, the one most often used in contests is
Safety. This subject, in turn, is divided into two parts—safety
in driving and safety elsewhere.

For your guidance in coming contests of this nature, consider
these three top prize winners in different safe-driving slogan
competitions:

Drive like lightning and you will crash like thunder.

This slogan won a $15,000 car plus $1,000 in cash in a contest conducted by Walter Winchell in behalf of the Damon Run-
you Cancer Fund. It is based on analogy—using the storm words,
"lightning" and "thunder."

Budget your speed after dark—live within your beams.

This won a deluxe sedan in General Motors' contest for a
slogan about driving at night. Like the Winchell winner, it is
based mainly on analogy, tying in the monetary word "budget"
with a parody on another pecuniary expression—"live within
your means."

Safety isn't measured by a broken rule.

A new car every year for life was awarded by Dodge for this
slogan, which employs double meaning and related words,
"measured" and "rule."

Other safe-driving slogans, including some major winners,
follow:

Wild dashes from by-ways cause crashes on highways.

Drive so your license expires before you do.

Big mistake many make—rely on horn instead of
brake.

Drivers seeking first rights sometimes get their last
rites.

Children should be seen and not hurt.

From bar to car to Gates Ajar.

Don't make safety first your last resort.

Hardly a driver is now alive who passed on hills at 75.

Slow down—death begins at 40.

Thinking drivers never drink—drinking drivers never think.

The shortest way to a hospital is through a red light.

Careful drivers are survivors.

Don't hug the car ahead—it's going steady.

Accidents lurk where brakes don't work.

Try saving lives instead of saving time.

Safety pays—speeders pay.

Drivers who think first, last!

General Safety Slogans

Don't take a chance—that chance may take you.

Alert today—alive tomorrow.

If you care to keep working, keep working with care.

Absence of accidents depends upon presence of mind.

Never be haphazard with a fire hazard.

Don't play in fun with a loaded gun.

When crossing streets, use your head and save your neck.

Don't be half safe—look both ways.

Fix carpet rip before you trip.

Play safe and you'll play longer.

Accidents are lamentable—but they're also preventable!

Give Yourself a Fair Test

A timely contest subject following publication of this book
will be the New York World's Fair of 1964 and 1965. Many big
prizes will surely be offered in connection with this outstanding event; and it is quite likely that some contests will call for
slogans about the Fair.

From the creative methods demonstrated in this chapter,
you should be able to devise suitable slogans based on the following information, taken from the Fair's own descriptive literature:

"Peace Through Understanding" is the theme of the New York
World's Fair. "Here the arts and ideas, products and progress
of the nations and peoples of the world will be gathered in a
memorable assembly of friendship, humanity and hope. . . .

"Under the symbol of the Unisphere, exhibits from all parts
of the world will be displayed for your delight. You'll visit
gleaming pavilions, wander through exotic temples and serene
gardens, tour towering fantasies of glass and steel. . . .

"You'll wonder at predictions of things to come, gaze at re-
creations of things past. You'll see water shows, theater pro-
ductions, circuses, sports events, fireworks, symphonies and
brass bands. In this Olympics of Progress, you will truly see
the best from all the world."

What sort of slogans can you weave from this material—slogans that will make people eager to visit and enjoy this spectacular exposition? Here's an example, in the author's own alliterative style:

See the Sixties' Scene Supreme!

As contest ads often say, you can do better than that. Try
it—to give yourself some good practice and a Fair chance of
winning!

Chapter 12

ANALOGY IN ACTION

After reading all foregoing chapters describing winning techniques, you will have observed that many methods appear repeatedly—having proved successful in every kind of contest cited so far.

While rhyme appears to be the most often used device in winning entries of all varieties, that method has been thoroughly covered in preceding pages and needs no further endorsement.

Analogy, however, which ranks next to rhyme as a specific winning factor, merits more attention than has been given to it before in this book. In fact, the author has good reason to acknowledge at this point the importance of analogy in winning a worth-while award.

Contest on Courtesy

Early in 1963, while these chapters were being written, a contest was conducted by the Transit Authority of New York City for best conclusions in no more than 50 words to this sentence:

> "It pays to be courteous on subways and T.A. buses
> because . . . "

Four top prizes were offered—each a week's vacation at the Condado Beach Hotel in San Juan, Puerto Rico, with round trip by Trans Caribbean Airways jet plane.

Three entries were submitted by the author, who, as a daily subway rider for many years, was well acquainted with the subject of this contest. One entry was in the form of a prose acrostic, based on the theme word, COURTESY:

C onsideration for
O ther passengers
U nquestionably
R epays us well—
T aking the rough
E dges off travel and
S moothing daily relations—
Y et courtesy costs nothing!

Another entry employed verse:

You can ride without fuss
In subway or bus
If you treat other riders politely;
Because when you do,
They'll be courteous, too—
Your right acts help the rest to act rightly.
So heed, when you ride,
The Golden Rule guide—
For daily it pays to be knightly!

The third entry was based on analogy, as indicated by the capitalized words:

Courtesy is the OIL that smooths the TRACKS
of daily travel, takes the FRICTION out of
crowded contacts, keeps all passengers in
pleasant GEAR, and lets the WHEELS of regular riding roll along with smiling, not riling,
results.

Analogy Pays Again

When the Transit Authority announced results of its courtesy
contest, the author was pleasantly surprised to be among the
top prize winners—but much more surprised to learn that his
winning entry was the one using analogy rather than his own favorite in verse!
One lesson which you may derive from reading of this experience is to <u>try several entries of various types whenever</u>

permitted by contest rules, since you cannot always trust your
own judgment of any single entry's winning potentiality.

Of more direct benefit, though, may be an account of how
analogy was employed to make this entry a grand prize winner.

How a Top Prize Was Won

As you will recall from recurrent advice in earlier chapters,
compiling lists of appropriate words is an essential preparation
to compose suitable entries in virtually every contest that you
may try, if it involves any form of creative writing.

For this particular Transit Authority contest, on the subject
of courtesy in bus and subway, two separate word lists seemed
to be required—one dealing with the mechanical or physical features of rapid transit, and the other with mental or emotional
attitudes toward such travel. When completed, these two lists
contained the following terms:

Transit Words

brake	fast	passenger	stand
bus	friction	platform	station
car	gear	rapid	token
carry	grease	ride	train
conductor	jostle	rider	transport
convenient	lubricate	roll	travel
crowd	motorman	seat	track
fare	oil	shove	wheel

Attitude Words

annoy	decent	manners	right
behave	fair	mutual	rile
bother	fuss	pleasant	rough
consideration	Golden Rule	polite	rude
contact	good will	practice	smile
courteous	harmony	relations	smooth
courtesy	impolite	respect	treat

There are two ways to create analogy entries from such lists. The first method is to utilize analogs that relate directly to your subject. This is what was done in the author's prize-winning entry in the Transit Authority contest.

Mulling over his two reference lists, he noticed that the word "friction" could apply equally well to mechanical action or human relations. How can friction be overcome? In machinery, by some form of lubrication, usually oil.

Among crowded passengers, courtesy would be the natural "oil" to reduce annoying friction. Addition of a few more analogs, such as tracks, gear, and wheels, with fitting phrases, resulted in construction of the quoted entry, which turned out to be a top prize winner.

Another Way to Use Analogy

The second way to compose entries based on analogy is to use words which belong to a different field, yet make sense when applied to your primary subject. For example, the word "platform" in the transit list might suggest an entry built around political analogs, like this:

> When Courtesy is the main PLANK in your
> PLATFORM, your CONVENTIONAL conduct
> will make you POPULAR with all PARTIES.

If that mythical entry sounds somewhat familiar, it's because a similar theme was used for another example of analogy in a beverage statement contest mentioned in Chapter 7.

You can see, then, how adaptable this second method is for almost every type of entry. To employ it most effectively when working on any new contest, you should have special lists of classified words in your files for ready reference.

Your classifications may include terms in just about any well-known field—art, music, acting, sport (in its manifold branches), financial, naval, military and scores of others.

How can such categories of analogs help you compose prize-worthy entries? Well, suppose you had to write on why you prefer to shop at some particular store—which is a perennial contest topic.

If you happen to be a typical consumer, you'd probably think
first of "quality with economy" as a good reason for dealing any-
where. But that in itself is too trite and obvious as the basis for
a contest entry. So you think a little deeper along that line—how
can you prove you're getting quality merchandise at thrifty prices?
Why, by checking values with similar offers in other stores.

Now the word "checking" stirs a new thought in your mind.
Recognizing it as a term used in chess, you look up your lists of
Game Analogs. Under "Chess and Checkers" you may find all
these related words:

advance	checkmate	expert	master
advantage	chess	file	mate
attack	chessman	force	menace
beat	color	forward	mobility
beginner	concentrate	gambit	movable
bishop	corner	game	move
block	counter	give up	objective
blunder	crown	guard	offense
board	defeat	hostile	opponent
capture	defend	interpose	opposition
caution	defense	jump	parry
castle	development	king	partner
challenge	diagonal	knight	pastime
champion	draw	lose	patience
check	enemy	man	pawn
checkers	exchange	maneuver	penalty
piece	remove	skill	tie
play	resign	square	tournament
position	retreat	stalemate	trap
problem	rook	strategy	victor
protect	row	tactics	win
queen	sacrifice	take	withdraw
rank	score	threat	yield

Rewarding Results

Choosing judiciously from this wealth of material, you can
soon create an unusual and outstanding entry of winning caliber,
incorporating several chess analogs, like this:

I prefer to shop at Food Fair because . . . by CHECK-
ING values, I've found my smartest MOVE was to Food
Fair, always on the SQUARE and above BOARD, pleas-
ing me and my MATE.

This entry example and collection of chess terms first appeared in Contest Magazine, as part of a series called "Analogy
Anthology," by the author of this book.

In the next chapter, you will learn all about Contest Magazine
and other "Sources of Success" which can prove of great benefit
to every earnest prize seeker.

Chapter 13

SOURCES OF SUCCESS

This volume is intended to cover every major field of creative writing for commercial contests as comprehensively as necessary for your complete information.

However, there is one vital element of this engrossing hobby which obviously cannot be included in any book. That phase would involve providing details of all new contests as they are announced, with specific assistance for each one of importance.

Only magazines or news bulletins, published every month or more often, can render such specialized, up-to-the-minute service for contestants.

Of course, you may encounter occasional ads announcing new contests through your favorite daily paper, general magazine, radio or TV program. But that's a hit-or-miss approach to contesting.

If you really wish to make this a profitable hobby, you'll want to keep abreast of all worth-while prize offers that appear at frequent intervals in many varied media.

Profitable Periodicals

To accomplish that purpose, you should get acquainted with some or all of the contest periodicals to be described in this chapter. After becoming familiar with the kind of help and information that they provide, you can then decide which of them would be likely to benefit you most as a regular subscriber. The following publications are listed in alphabetical order:

Contest Magazine

Published every month since 1928, Contest Magazine is not only the oldest but also the most popular periodical in its field.

It is a digest-sized magazine, averaging 80 pages per issue, well printed on slick paper, with pictures and extra colors on the cover and inside. In keeping with its attractive appearance is the consistently high caliber of its contents, which contest hobbyists find so helpful every month.

This long-standing record of reliability as an aid for prize seekers has made Contest Magazine the "bible" of regular winners and would-be winners alike. Their esteem is also based on the wide range of subjects presented in each issue, which contains such features as these:

Complete listings of all current contests, with every detail needed for entering.

Articles by expert winners and specialists in various types of competition, analyzing the requirements of the latest contests and suggesting ways to win them.

"The Entry Clinic," a department conducted by Charles A. Kraatz, noted prize winner and contest teacher, criticizing readers' unsuccessful entries and showing improved versions.

Reports of local and regional contests.

Compilations of related words and phrases to serve as idea starters in composition of entries.

A department devoted to contest fans who like to correspond with one another by way of "Round Robins," or group letters.

Advice by a Certified Public Accountant, Joseph Arkin, on how to prepare proper tax reports on prizes won in contests.

News about the doings of contest clubs in cities throughout the country, conventions of Statewide or regional hobby organizations, and reports of the activities of the National Contesters Association—of which you will learn more later in this chapter.

Contest Magazine is published by A. D. Freese & Sons, Inc., Upland, Indiana, and edited by Hugh Freese. A single copy of the latest issue may be ordered for fifty cents. The regular subscription rate is $4.50 for one year; but a trial subscription is available at $1.00 for three monthly issues.

Contest Worksheet

This bulletin is published twice a month by Art Reiss, P.O. Box 4027, Dallas 8, Texas. It contains news, tips, and comments on current and coming contests, suitable word lists, winning entries and answers to questions about contests. Single copy price, 35 cents. Trial subscription, $1.25 for two months (four issues).

Eggleston Enterprize

Published monthly by Niles Eggleston, Milford, New York, this bulletin offers timely news of contests and related services. Single copy, 15 cents; $1.50 per year.

General Contest Bulletin

A monthly publication edited by G. P. Pederson, 1609 East Fifth St., Duluth 12, Minnesota. Contains news, articles, questions and answers about contests. Single copy, 25 cents; $2.50 per year.

Prize Ideas

Bearing the slogan, "Your Guide to Winner Wonderland," this bulletin is published twice a month by the All-American School, 1429 Spruce St., Philadelphia 2, Pa. It is edited by the school's director, Charles A. Kraatz.

Under the skillful guidance of Mr. Kraatz, Prize Ideas has been a source of "winspiration" to its readers ever since it started publication in 1938, when the All-American School was established. You will understand why when you examine a copy of this bulletin. In a typical issue, you will find such helpful features as these:

> Full details of the latest national contests offering attractive prizes, along with reports of worth-while regional contests. How-to-win advice specifically slanted for outstanding current contests. Two entire pages of entries that have won prizes in recent national, regional and local contests. Coverage of radio and

TV prize offers. Ad excerpts to stimulate entry ideas. Success stories by major prize winners.

On request to the All-American School, you will receive a free copy of Prize Ideas, giving subscription rates, and information about the school's Correspondence Course in Contest Winning.

Shepherd Confidential Contest Bulletin

Issued every other week, this bulletin is edited by Buell R. Snyder and published by the Shepherd School, 1015 Chestnut St., Philadelphia 7, Pa.

This school—known in full as the Shepherd Correspondence School of Contest Technique—was founded in 1931 by Wilmer S. Shepherd, Jr., who is responsible for the winning lessons and special features that make his course and bulletin so popular and effective.

Mr. Shepherd is famous in the contest field for imbuing his students with the spirit and knowledge that have made so many of them notably successful in capturing major prizes. His exceptional talent for conveying the ability to win is manifest in every issue of his Confidential Contest Bulletin.

Its slogan, "Shears for the Golden Fleece," graphically and accurately describes the aims and accomplishments of the Shepherd Bulletin, as attested by the great number of winning entries published therein.

Write to the Shepherd School for a free copy of this bulletin, with information regarding its availability, and for details of the Shepherd Coaching Course in Contest Winning.

What's Cooking in Contests

Published monthly by Robert Spence Publications, Inc., 1315 Central Ave., St. Petersburg, Florida. Edited by Edward L. Lee. This magazine specializes in puzzle contests, featuring analytical articles by William Sunners, who is a nationally recognized expert in that field. Single copy, 35 cents. Trial subscription, $1.00 for three months.

Of the seven publications described here, you will note that two—Prize Ideas and the Shepherd Bulletin—definitely offer one issue free to anyone requesting it. With the exception of Contest Magazine, the other periodicals listed will probably send you a sample copy without charge, if you mention the source of your request—as should be done when asking for complimentary copies of any publication.

Though Contest Magazine does not supply free copies for examination, you can be sure of getting your money's worth when taking a trial subscription to that periodical, since it is unquestionably the outstanding publication in the prize-pursuing pastime.

If your interest in contests includes literary as well as commercial prize offers, any of the following monthly magazines will serve to keep you well informed of purely literary competitions:

Author & Journalist, P.O. Box 1914, Denver 1, Colorado. Single copy, 35 cents; $4.00 per year.

The Writer, 8 Arlington St., Boston 16, Mass. Single copy, 40 cents; $5.00 per year.

Writer's Digest, 22 East 12th St., Cincinnati 10, Ohio. Single copy, 35 cents; $4.00 per year.

All three of these magazines will send a sample copy upon request.

Tools of the Trade

If contest periodicals may be considered "Sources of Success"—as indeed they are—then equally worthy of mention in this category are the other implements needed by contesters to pursue their hobby in the most efficient manner possible. Such "tools of the trade" should include some or all of the following books (besides this one, of course!):

The latest edition of any standard dictionary—preferably an abridged version that is comprehensive but not too cumbersome for ready reference.

A thesaurus of synonyms and antonyms. An excellent modern

edition of Roget's Thesaurus is available in pocket size for
only 50 cents.

A rhyming dictionary. Books of this type by Burgess Johnson,
Langford Reed, and Clement Wood are much alike in scope
and arrangement, and equally valuable for convenient consultation. The Walker-Dawson edition is designed differently,
not quite as easy to use, but with word definitions as well as
rhymes.

A volume of quotations, proverbs, and familiar sayings.

A book of famous poems, and another of nursery rhymes (for
style and parody).

Compilations of jokes, anecdotes and humorous verse.

Collections of popular limericks, such as those edited by Bennett
Cerf and Louis Untermeyer.

While most books of this kind are available for borrowing or
reference at public libraries, you will find it much more convenient to possess your own copies for handy consultation at
home. Properly utilized, they can help you win prizes that will
soon repay their cost—plus plenty of profit.

Such volumes are obtainable through local book dealers; or
you may write to Freese Publications, Upland, Indiana, for a
free catalog of many books and pamphlets specially selected to
benefit contesters in their quest for prizes.

More Tools for Mining Contest Gold

In addition to helpful books and magazines, what other equipment should you have in your Winning Workshop? Not every-
thing that follows is essential; but all are desirable items.

You should keep on hand a supply of good quality writing
paper, for entries that are not required to be submitted on official blanks. Envelopes should be large enough to take your
entries without folding more than twice. Index cards, 3 x 5 inches
in size, are quite suitable for short entries, and fit into even
small envelopes.

Plain white cards or paper can make attractive entries if
properly prepared; but if you prefer to use lightly tinted stationery, no contest judge is likely to object to it.

Clear-writing, non-smudging pens in various colors should

be available for appropriate usage; but your signature should always be in discreet blue or black ink.

A small loose-leaf notebook, which can be carried around handily, will serve well for recording stray thoughts on current contests, as they occur to you. Such random ideas can later be worked into full-fledged entries, when you have access to your complete file of reference material.

An asset to any contester is a typewriter, preferably with elite or small type, rather than pica, which is somewhat larger. Reason: When required entry blanks do not allow much writing space, you can get more words in the same area with smaller type. However, if you have a pica typewriter and your letters overflow the given space, it is generally permissible to paste a piece of paper to the blank and finish your entry thereon. Your typewriter should be equipped with a red-and-black ribbon, to permit an emphatic touch of color in strategic spots.

While typewritten entries may be favored for legibility by some contest judges, it is not necessary to type your entries in order to win—unless the rules so specify. Thousands of contestants have won major prizes with entries that were neatly and clearly printed or written by hand.

Filing for the Future

Aside from its legibility, a typewriter has one important advantage for contestants over handwriting—it makes better carbon copies, for more convenient filing.

If you are completely new to the contest hobby, you may wonder why it is advisable to make and keep carbon copies of your entries. The best answer is simply—Reference Value. By saving all past entries, you will gradually accumulate a rich storehouse of your own material that may be reworked, refined, and reused in future contests, whether or not such entries won before.

Another good reason for keeping copies of your entries is to compare them with published winners in the same contests, to see what improvements may be needed in efforts that may have failed to win. Such comparisons can often prove exceedingly helpful in showing you what it takes to capture a prize.

For filing copies of your own entries, as well as contest ads, bulletins, and other pertinent data, you should use manila file folders, available at any stationery store. At the start of your contesting career, a table or desk drawer may be sufficient to store this material; but eventually you will want a regular filing cabinet—which can be paid for out of your winnings in due time.

Twelve Typical Toppers

So far, this chapter has covered such sources of success in contesting as books, magazines, and other "tools of the trade"— all valuable, all important, but all inanimate.

To many contesters, though, the most inspiring wellspring of success is the positive knowledge that other people like themselves have achieved fame and fortune in the same field of endeavor.

"What they can do, I can do!" That enthusiastic emotion is the magic key that unlocks the door of doubt and lets you enter the vault of victory. And what could be more evocative of such enthusiasm than to learn what other people have won, who they are, and where they live? Listed here are just a few noteworthy winners—an even dozen selected from various parts of the country—whose prize attainments may well encourage you to keep trying until similar success comes your way.

ALABAMA: Mrs. Lillou McCain of Birmingham won two cars from General Mills, and $5,000 from Procter & Gamble, among other prizes.

CALIFORNIA: Mrs. Nita Parks of Pasadena has won more than $40,000 in prizes, including one of $25,000 for a last line in a Colgate jingle contest.

COLORADO: Mrs. Sybil Todd of Denver won two overseas vacation trips within a single year, one to Europe and the other to the Orient.

FLORIDA: Mrs. Nancy Ungaro of North Miami won $30,000 for a statement about a Zenith television set.

MINNESOTA: Mrs. Deborah Schneider of Minneapolis won $500 a month for life for 25 words about Plymouth cars.

MISSOURI: Mrs. Grace Ellen Tousley of Independence won her

weight in gold—amounting to exactly $50,318.06—for a state-
ment about the Easy Combomatic Washer-Dryer.

NORTH CAROLINA: Stanford Mizelle of Raleigh won $25,000 in
a Colgate picture title contest.

OHIO: Albert M. Husted of Cincinnati won three automobiles in
less than one year in statement and slogan contests.

OKLAHOMA: Dale Kelly of Oklahoma City won a month's vacation with his family at a chateau on the French Riviera in
Gulf Oil's jingle contest.

OREGON: Mrs. Dorette Lemon of Portland won free food for
life (at the rate of $25 worth a week) in a Betty Crocker-
Sunkist contest for naming a pie "Lemon Dorette"—a trans-
position of her own name!

TEXAS: Donald Parkinson of Dallas, grand prize winner in a
Dial Soap jingle contest, was given his choice of $25,000
cash or the income from an active oil well. He took the cash
award.

WASHINGTON: George Hill of Seattle has won more than 2,600
separate prizes in his long contest career—and he's still going strong!

Comradeship in Contesting

To read about these contest stars and their amazing accomplishments is indeed thrilling to prize seekers who aspire to
similar goals. Even more thrilling to many contest fans would
be a chance to meet some famous winners in person, talk to
them, and hear them relate their own success stories. If such
encounters appeal to you, by all means join the National Contesters Association, where comradeship is the keynote.

This organization, whose aim is to have "Every member a
winner and every winner a member," was founded in 1937 by
Everett Lane, of Fredericksburg, Virginia. Since then, NCA
(as the association is known in the contest field) has held annual conventions in different cities throughout the nation.

NCA conventions are attended by several hundred enthusiastic prize pursuers every year, eager to hear words of wisdom
from outstanding winners, teachers, editors, judges, sponsors,
advertising specialists, and other people prominent in the con-

test world. Recent conventions were held in New York, 1960;
St. Louis, 1961; Miami Beach, 1962; and Denver, 1963; with
Los Angeles scheduled for 1964 and San Antonio for 1965.

In addition to the sociability and mutual assistance it offers
all members, NCA has a particularly worthy purpose—to bring
the benefits of the contest hobby to shut-in or handicapped people, including hospitalized war veterans. To such "Winsiders,"
as NCA calls them, this engrossing pastime offers not only
monetary but therapeutic rewards.

The latest information about NCA appears every month in
Contest Magazine, or may be obtained directly from any of
these current officers:

Mrs. Pauline Bruer   Mrs. Etta V. Fogerty
807 North 41st Avenue   5014 Shrewsbury Avenue
Omaha 31, Nebraska   Webster Groves 19, Missouri

Mrs. Sibyl Todd   Mr. Jay Wrinkle
1095 South Fillmore Way   3636 Lansing Avenue
Denver 9, Colorado   Knoxville 14, Tennessee

A self-addressed stamped envelope or return postage should
always be enclosed when requesting a reply.

While NCA is the only nationwide organization for contest
fans, there are several regional associations of prize seekers,
which conduct their own conventions. Many cities have contest
clubs that hold monthly meetings, where newcomers to this
hobby are as welcome as regular winners. Full details about
all these local and regional groups also appear in every issue
of Contest Magazine.

So, you see, there are many sources of success in the won-
drous world of contesting—books, magazines, societies—with
inspiration for individual achievement to be found in all of them.

Chapter 14

PATTERNS FOR PROFIT

Long-experienced prize winners, who have followed the contest hobby for many years, can skip this little chapter without missing anything not already known to them.

However, for newcomers to what has been aptly called "the pastime that pays," the subject briefly treated here should prove both revealing and rewarding. It will cover certain well-known winning ways, not previously mentioned because of their rather limited effectiveness.

These patterns, formulas or entry designs—as they are variously termed—have been used by knowing contestants in countless competitions with consistent success. In fact, such forms have been employed so many times that some of them have become recognizable from repetition, and can no longer capture major prizes in national contests.

Limited to Locals

Nevertheless, winning entries published in the very latest contest bulletins demonstrate beyond a doubt that even the most familiar versions of patterned entries still continue to win regularly in local contests—and occasionally in those of broader scope.

Perhaps there is more prestige in winning a national contest prize than a local award. But, as Gertrude Stein might have said, a car is a car is a car—and a brand new Cadillac presented to you by a neighborhood merchant in a community contest is worth just as much as if you had won it in a highly publicized nationwide competition sponsored by General Motors itself. And, of course, a thousand dollars in cash is a "grand" award—no matter who gives it to you.

Take Your Pick!

So, whenever you are tempted to try a contest confined to
your own home town or shopping area, the following formulas
will facilitate your entry writing—especially in composing short
statements—for they help to organize your thoughts along certain lines that seem to find perennial favor with judges of local-
ly limited prize offers.

When rules of such community contests allow you to submit
more than a single entry in the same competition, it would be
generally advisable to include your choice of some of these po-
tentially profitable patterns, since you never can tell when your
"pick" may strike gold!

Admire-Desire-Require Form

(This is the grandpa of all prize patterns—but there's life in the
old boy yet!)

My favorite store features styles I <u>admire</u>, products I
<u>desire,</u> and bargains I <u>require</u>.

This paint provides the finish I <u>admire</u>, the surface I
<u>desire,</u> and the durability I <u>require</u>.

Alphabet Form

Filled with healthful vitamins, this food gives me a
"B"-eneficial meal with "D"-elightful taste and "G"-
enerous supply of "E"-nergy.

To men who mind their tobacco P's and Q's, this
cigar makes smoking satisfaction as simple as A, B, C.

I've found them best by every test from "A"-roma
clear to "Z"-est.

Arithmetic Form

This shoe polish <u>adds</u> new appearance, <u>subtracts</u> scuff
marks, and <u>multiplies</u> life of footwear.

This shortening <u>adds</u> delicious flavor, <u>subtracts</u> greasiness, <u>divides</u> food costs, and <u>multiplies</u> mealtime pleasure.

Ease and E's Form

This car combines EASE of driving with the E's of Efficiency, Economy and Excellence—satisfying Everyone.

Extra Form

This cigaret is <u>extra</u> long, <u>extra</u> mild, <u>extra</u> cool—at no <u>extra</u> cost.

Five Senses Form

I can <u>see</u> this bread's purity; <u>feel</u> its fine texture; <u>smell</u> its wheaty fragrance; <u>taste</u> its fresh flavor; and <u>hear</u> my family praise it.

Healthy-Wealthy-Wise Form

I can be <u>healthy</u> with this soda's purity, <u>wealthy</u> saving on its quantity, and <u>wise</u> in choosing such delicious refreshment.

I'm mouth <u>healthy</u> and tooth <u>wealthy</u> because I'm <u>wise</u> enough to use this dentifrice.

Kind Form

This cigar is <u>kind</u> to my throat; <u>kind</u> to my tongue; and <u>kind</u> to my wallet—therefore, it's my <u>kind</u> of smoke.

Password Form

This syrup is the <u>password</u> to eager appetites; the <u>watchword</u> for wholesome energy; the <u>buy-word</u> for economy; and the <u>last word</u> for flavor.

This store is the <u>password</u> to variety; the <u>watchword</u>
for reliability; the <u>buy-word</u> for bargains; and the
<u>last word</u> in obliging service.

Pledge of Allegiance Form

This beverage pledges allegiance to good taste and to
the purity with which it's made—one flavor individual
with energizing effect upon all.

Satisfy Both Form

When my pride demands Class, and my bankbook demands Thrift, I <u>satisfy both</u> with this elegant yet inexpensive car.

When hunger urges me to dine out, and my wallet
warns me to wait, I <u>satisfy both</u> at this popular-priced
restaurant.

Singular Form

It's truly a <u>singular</u> candy—<u>one</u> quality: the highest—
<u>one</u> flavor: the tastiest—and <u>one</u> price: the thriftiest!

Stop-Look-Listen Form

Since I use this toothpaste, my friends <u>stop,</u> they <u>look,</u>
and I <u>listen</u> to compliments on my brighter teeth.

Universal Form

This product puts a premium on perfection, a seal on
satisfaction, and an emphasis on economy.

A Word to the Wise

When using any of the patterns shown in this chapter, you
must remember that they are already familiar to many con-

testants—and will become known to many more through their
publication here.

So, while you may feel free to follow whatever designs you
prefer, do not copy any quoted example word for word. Instead,
try to originate your own apt expressions to fit the given frame-
work.

Thereby, you can turn entries that were trite into entries
that are bright—the kind judges take a shine to every time!

Chapter 15

SPEAKING TO SPONSORS

Sponsors of successful prize contests—who are far too numerous to be named here individually—certainly need no advice from the author of this book.

To such sponsors—some of whom were mentioned in preceding chapters—the writer can only express deep and earnest gratitude. They have given him and hosts of other contest fans the most fascinating hobby on earth—one that is based on the fundamental emotion of Hope.

Skeptics may scoffingly quote the Biblical line, "Hope deferred maketh the heart sick"—and it cannot be denied that the hope of winning a major prize is more often deferred than fulfilled for most contestants.

However, another adage of equal truth and greater potency may be cited more optimistically in this connection—"Hope springs eternal in the human breast."

The Hobby Built on Hope

There can be no doubt that contests hold out hope of rich rewards and a better life for millions of people whose future would otherwise appear drab, humdrum and routine. There is a powerful, stimulating allure in the prospect of attaining sudden fame and fortune by placing first in a national contest offering huge, entrancing awards.

It matters not that the sponsor's motive for running contests is to boost his business and to make bigger profits. To the eager entrant, a contest's product is less important than its by-product—which is the hope it arouses of winning a sensational prize.

Hence, all prize seekers should be grateful—and most of

them are—to the sponsors whose continuous contests serve
(even if only incidentally) to nurture the entrants' eternal hope
of achieving some spectacular success through this hobby which
offers not only the pursuit of happiness, but the happiness of
pursuit.

Pointers for Prospective Sponsors

While the author frankly admits that he has nothing but heart-
felt thanks to offer long-established and widely-experienced contest sponsors, his purpose in this chapter goes beyond that. His
aim here is threefold:

1. To explain the value of well-conducted creative contests to business executives who have never before
   employed this effective means of sales promotion.

2. To refer such prospective sponsors to organizations
   which specialize in handling all phases of contests.

3. To recommend publications which may yield further
   information relating to contest sponsorship.

How Creative Contests Can Benefit Your Business

The surest way to familiarize more consumers with your
product or service is to run a prize contest requiring entrants
to write about that particular subject. It makes little difference
whether the entry is in the form of a statement, slogan or
jingle—so long as it deals directly with your product.

The lasting value of this type of promotion has been con-
firmed through thousands of contests which attracted many millions of entrants. A satisfyingly large proportion of these contestants became regular customers after once testing a product in order to write about it convincingly for a possible prize.

Taking a tip from these facts, a new contest sponsor should
always insist upon entries that actually describe the virtues of
his product. Unquestionably, that is the best way to turn a contest trier into a steady buyer.

Other Advantages of Prize Promotion

Increasing the sales of your product by attracting new customers is probably the greatest advantage you can expect from
any contest. However, there are many other ways in which contests may benefit your business. Here are some of the purposes
they can serve:

Gain attention for a newly introduced product.

Find new uses for an established product.

Assure prominent product display by dealers.

Open new territory, especially through a regional
contest.

Induce consumers to visit dealers for a demonstration (if your product calls for such action).

Develop a reliable mailing list of current prospects.

Obtain a usable slogan or new name for a product.

Reveal, through keyed entry coupons, which of your
advertising media pulled best.

Improve public relations and build good will.

Overcome seasonal sales slumps.

Offset other types of campaigns by competitors.

Mark a special occasion, such as your company's
25th anniversary—or even its first.

Announce improvements in your product.

Secure testimonials for advertising use, describing how your product benefits consumers.

Why Professional Assistance Is Advisable

To get the fullest value from a contest, while avoiding a
lot of extra work, trouble and unforeseen expenses, you

should secure the services of a reputable professional contest judging company.

Such firms are employed by most commercial contest sponsors, including every one whose name is nationally recognized—which accounts in great part for the success and regular repetition of their popular prize promotions.

As a prospective contest sponsor, you would do well to follow the same procedures that have been used to such advantage in this field so far. Experienced sponsors know that there are several sound reasons for hiring a professional judging agency to handle their contests. Among these reasons are the following:

1. The sponsoring company cannot be accused of showing partiality in the selection of prize winners.
2. Any resentment that might be felt by non-winners would be directed against the judging organization rather than the sponsor.
3. Reputable judging companies are insured to cover mistakes or claims of any kind likely to arise.
4. Neither sponsors nor their advertising agencies are equipped to handle the overwhelming flood of mailed entries—often numbering more than a million separate pieces—drawn by a big contest.
5. Even if all contest mail could be physically handled by the sponsor's own staff, they lack the proper qualifications to evaluate entries according to the strict standards set by Post Office regulations.
6. A professional judging organization can help the sponsor plan his contest from its very inception, taking into consideration his particular merchandising problems.
7. The specially trained staff of a professional judging service provides competent evaluation of all entries on an objective, impersonal basis, assuring absolute fairness to all contestants.
8. Expert appraisal of entries by qualified judges will eliminate errors in selection which could prove costly and embarrassing.
9. From long experience, a professional judging organization knows how to handle legitimate queries

or complaints from entrants, as well as the crank
mail which some contests occasionally evoke.

Where to Find Help in Conducting Your Contest

In most large cities, organizations which offer professional
contest judging service are listed in the Yellow Pages of tele-
phone directories. Rather oddly, they appear under different
classifications in various cities' phone books.

In the Manhattan classified directory of New York City—
where most of these services are located—you will find them
under the heading, "Sales Contest Organizers," which also
covers prize suppliers and promotional consultants.

Among the judging organizations listed here are the following "Big Three," which handle most of the largest national contests:

> Advertising Distributors of America, Inc., 400
> Madison Ave., New York 17, N.Y.

> D. L. Blair Corp., 38 East 29th St., New York 16, N.Y.

> Reuben H. Donnelley Corp., 230 East Sandford Blvd.,
> Mount Vernon, N.Y.

Some other companies listed under the same heading do not
offer judging service, but will supply trips, cars, and other attractive merchandise prizes for your contest at minimum cost.
Three of these firms are:

> Marden-Kane, Inc., 666 Fifth Ave., New York 19, N.Y.

> S. Jay Reiner Co., Inc., 155 Mineola Blvd., Mine-
> ola, L.I., N.Y.

> V. I. P. Service, Inc., 720 Fifth Ave., New York 19, N.Y.

Similar or related service is offered by other companies
which appear under the headings "Premium Goods" and "Premium Service," including:

Contest Premiums, Inc., 386 Park Ave., South,
New York 16, N.Y.

Kayrill Enterprises, 150 Fifth Ave., New York 11,
N.Y.

R. L. Polk & Co., 60 East 56th St., New York 22,
N.Y. (This company is also a well-known national
contest judging organization, with headquarters
in Chicago, as noted hereinafter.)

Under a different category—"Business Counselors"—appears
the name of another specialist in contest consultation: Stanley
Arnold & Associates, Inc., 375 Park Ave., New York 22, N.Y.
Listed under "Sales Promotion and Counseling Service" is
Zenn Kaufman, 420 Lexington Ave., New York 17, N.Y. Mr.
Kaufman is the author of the best book ever written expressly
for commercial contest sponsors. Called Successful Prize Contests, this volume of more than 500 fact-packed pages was published in 1951 by Prentice-Hall, Inc.

In Philadelphia's Yellow Pages, the classification to look for
is "Sales Promotional Service." Among other firms, the Donnelley organization appears again here, at 401 N. Broad Street.

In Chicago, under the specific heading, "Contest Judging,"
the classified directory lists these three companies, which also
operate in other cities.

Advertising Distributors of America, Inc., 250
West 87th Street.

Reuben H. Donnelley Corp., 2000 York Road, Oak
Brook, Illinois.

R. L. Polk & Co., 333 West Lake Street.

In Detroit, under the same classification of "Contest Judging," the phone book lists two of the preceding firm names
again: Advertising Distributors at 4444 Cass Street; and R. L.
Polk at 431 Howard Street.

In Saint Paul, Minnesota, under "Sales Promotion Service,"
contest judging is offered by Spotts Mailing Corp., 2402 Uni-
versity Avenue.

In the Yellow Pages of Los Angeles, under the classification,

"Advertising—Direct Mail," may be found still another listing
for the contest service of Reuben H. Donnelley Corp., at 4632
Santa Monica Boulevard.

As a prospective contest sponsor, you will find your inquiries
welcomed by any of the judging services, consultants or prize
suppliers operating throughout the country, whether they are
mentioned here or not.

While you may find it convenient to deal with an agency
nearest your own business headquarters, even distantly located
organizations can serve you well, once your particular needs
are known to them.

Recommended Reading for Sponsors

For current information on the entire field of contest sponsorship, in all its varied phases and frequently changing as-
pects, you should read several of the following publications
regularly:

Advertisers Confidential Contest News Bulletin, published
    bimonthly by D. L. Blair Corp., 38 East 29th St., New York
    16, N.Y. Issued free to qualified applicants.
Advertising Age, 740 Rush Street, Chicago 11, Ill. Published
    weekly. Single copy, 25 cents; $5.00 per year.
Advertising & Sales Promotion, 740 Rush Street, Chicago 11,
    Ill. Published monthly. Single copy, 50 cents; $3.00 per
    year.
Incentive, 111 Fourth Avenue, New York 3, N.Y. Published
    monthly. Single copy, 50 cents; $4.00 per year.
Incentive Merchandising, 630 Third Avenue, New York 17, N.Y.
    Published monthly. Single copy, 50 cents; $5.00 per year.
Premium Merchandising, 521 Fifth Avenue, New York 17,
    N.Y. Published monthly. Single copy, 25 cents; $2.50 per
    year.
Printers' Ink, 635 Madison Avenue, New York 22, N.Y. Pub-
    lished weekly. Single copy 35 cents; $6.00 per year.
Reporter of Direct Mail Advertising, 224 Seventh St.,
    Garden City, Long Island, N. Y. Published monthly.
    Single copy, 75 cents; $7.50 per year.

Sales Management, 630 Third Avenue, New York 17, N.Y. Pub-
lished twice monthly. Single copy, 75 cents; $12.00 per year.
Sponsor, 555 Fifth Avenue, New York 17, N.Y. Published weekly.
Single copy, 40 cents; $8.00 per year.

Sample copies of these publications may be available if requested by executives on their company's letterhead.

A Last Word to Likely Sponsors

If you have never conducted a contest before to improve your
business, increase your sales and impress the public, now is
the time to try this profitable form of promotion, when you can
call upon so many special services to assist you in creating
contest themes, working up prize structures, receiving and
judging entries, selecting winners, and distributing awards.

Chapter 16

PRIZE PROBLEMS AND ANSWERS

What questions about contesting came to your mind as you read through this book? There is a good chance that you will find your individual prize problems—or at least something closely akin to them—discussed in this concluding chapter.

From long experience in answering queries from readers of his contest features in various magazines, the author has become familiar with the questions that seem to perplex most prize seekers. These standard inquiries, along with others that relate to special phases of the contest hobby, will be answered here.

Q. In a limerick or jingle contest, should I submit only my last line or copy the given lines and add my own?

A. If you use your own paper instead of an entry blank, it is better to copy the whole verse, adding your line about an inch or two below the other lines to make your entry stand out. Then leave more clear space under your line before filling in your name and address, and any dealer information that may be required.

Q. Some entry blanks say "write" your name, others say "sign" or "print." What's the difference?

A. The difference can be between getting a prize or not, since <u>rules must be followed exactly.</u> When asked to "write" or "sign" your name, your actual signature in longhand is wanted. "Print" means lettering either by hand or with a typewriter. For writing or printing, a pen is always preferable to a pencil. Even when typing, it's a good idea to SIGN your name by hand, to give your entry a personal touch.

Q. Are contractions like "isn't" or "she'll" considered as one word or two by contest judges?

A. While some published winning entries indicate that judges are not too strict on this point, it is safer to count contractions as TWO words, which they really are.

Q. May I send more than one entry to any contest?

A. If the rules do not definitely limit you to one entry, you may submit as many entries as you wish, provided each one is "qualified" by whatever proof-of-purchase that may be required. However, it is better to use a separate envelope for each entry, instead of putting several in the same envelope.

Q. When rules allow the use of either entry blanks or plain paper, which is preferable?

A. If the entry blank is crowded with printed matter and limited in writing space, plain paper would let you present your entry more neatly and attractively.

Q. What should I do when in doubt as to what part of a box is the actual top, since the product name does not always appear there?

A. Send the entire front, back or side of the box along with the opening flap, so there can be no mistake about it.

Q. When contest rules say all entries become the sponsor's property, does it mean we cannot even use our non-winners again?

A. That rule has no such significance. Sponsors use the phrase "all entries become our property" to avoid demands for return of material that failed to win—not to prevent you from using the same entries elsewhere. That's why you should always keep copies of whatever you submit to a contest—a good idea that once was a flopper may next time be a topper!

Q. When told to "enclose" a box top or label, should I clip, staple, or paste it to my entry?

A. Never paste or staple the qualifier to your entry, which could easily be torn or damaged by its removal. A clip may be used, but it must be kept away from the upper part of your en-

velope, to avoid damage during cancellation at the post office.
Your safest procedure is to enclose the qualifier loosely, without any attachment to your entry.

Q. I've noticed that addresses for the same contest are
given differently in newspaper ads, magazine ads, and entry
blanks. Which address should I use?
A. It doesn't really matter, since all entries for a specific
contest will reach the same judging destination, regardless of
minor variations in address. Different box numbers or initials
are used only to let the sponsor know where his contest ads
were seen.

Q. In a daily contest, may I repeat the same entry on different days?
A. Certainly. If you have composed what you consider a
good entry, it's worth trying several times when non-winning
entries are discarded after each day's judging is over. Remember, though, that this applies only to contests which award prizes
on a daily, weekly or monthly basis. For contests having but one
definite closing date, you should never repeat the same entry—
since duplicated material cannot win.

Q. Would joining a contest club help me to win more prizes?
A. Possibly. Many people succeed in winning consistently
without ever joining any contest clubs. Yet others derive great
benefit from social contact with fellow contestants. There's a
lot of fun in sharing the same hobby with friends. By exchanging
contest news and information, you may find such contacts profitable as well as pleasant.

Q. Is it O.K. to use slang words in entries?
A. If appropriate to the subject, there should be no objec-
tion; but avoid using any questionable term, like the entrant who
tried to praise a girdle by saying it could be removed easily by
a "short yank or a little jerk."

Q. When submitting statement entries on plain paper, should
I include the starting phrase given by the sponsor?
A. Yes, this is definitely desirable, since your entry must

form a complete sentence in conjunction with its beginning. However, the starting phrase does NOT count in the total number of
words allowed.

Q. If I win a prize after sending several entries to a contest,
is there any way I can learn which one of my entries won?
A. Usually, such information will not be disclosed by the
sponsor, no matter how nicely you may ask for it. But you can
"key" your entries to reveal which won by signing your name in
slightly different ways on each entry submitted—as: Mary
Brown, Mary J. Brown, Mrs. John Brown, Mrs. J. C. Brown,
Mary Jane Brown, and so on. Then, when a prize notification
comes your way, you can check its name style against your keyed
entry copies to identify the actual winner.

Q. When submitting opinion-type questions to TV or radio
programs, should I include some kind words for the sponsoring
product?
A. Better not. Such prize offers are made only to get usable
material. Additional remarks are unnecessary, and might even
spoil your chances of winning if the judges felt that you were
just trying to curry favor with your praise.

Q. What is meant by a "restricted entry"?
A. If contest sponsors do not want winning entries revealed
for publication, they may require winners to withhold that information. Under such conditions, entries are said to be "restricted." In some cases, only major prize winning entries are barred
from disclosure. However, many sponsors make no restrictions
of any sort even on entries that have won top awards.

Q. In naming contests, are duplicated entries always discarded?
A. They would be if the contest called for a name alone.
However, if an explanatory statement is required, duplicated
names may win according to the merit of the accompanying
reasons.

Q. Some contests ask for entries on postal cards. Would
it be all right to enclose such card entries in envelopes for

mailing, to keep them from being soiled by handling while in transit?

A. When rules require entries to be submitted on postal cards, anything submitted to the contest address in an envelope may be thrown away unopened and unread, since it would be considered a violation of the rules.

Q. What can be done when entry blanks are necessary but not available from dealers?

A. In that case, the only thing to do is to write directly to the sponsor of the contest, explain the situation, and ask for a few blanks by mail. Be sure to provide a stamped envelope addressed to yourself, with your request. You can always find the sponsor's address on the contest product.

Q. In statement contests calling for "25 words or less," how much "less" would be acceptable to the judges?

A. Generally, you should try to utilize most of the words allowed—not going below fifteen at least, or it may seem that you don't have enough good things to say about the product. However, an exceptionally clever idea might be expressed best in very few words; and such brevity may impress the judges favorably once in a while.

Q. Does it ever help to send in fancy or decorated entries? If so, how can it be done best?

A. There is no use wasting your time and effort to decorate entries in national contests, where ornamentation means nothing.

In local contests, though, which are generally handled by nonprofessional judges, some appropriate embellishment of your entry might tip the balance in your favor after all other factors have been evaluated. Decoration is usually done by illustrating entries with cartoons or sketches to fit their subject matter.

Contestants who lack artistic ability for original drawings manage well enough with pictures clipped from magazines, comic sections, and similar sources. It would be advisable to start a file of such cut-outs under various headings like Sports, Children, Couples, Landmarks, Home Scenes, Transportation, and many others likely to prove useful. Then, when a local contest is announced for which you consider decoration suitable, just pick an appropriate picture from your collection and work it into your entry.

You may even find that your "art gallery" will serve to stimulate new ideas and help you create something really unusual—which is the way to win.

Q. When dealer's name is requested on a contest blank, does it mean the name of the store, the owner or the clerk?

A. If the owner's name is part of the store name—like Greenbaum's Grocery—use it in just that form. If the store has an impersonal title, such as Thrifty Market, use that plus the name of the owner, manager, or clerk who filled your order.

Q. Would I have to pay income tax on any prize I won in a contest, even if it isn't in cash?

A. Yes. To quote from a recently published statement by officials of the Internal Revenue Service: "Prizes and awards are generally taxable and the fair market value must be included in gross income on tax returns. Prizes and awards which are reportable include, but are not limited to, amounts received from radio and television give-away shows, contests, door prizes, raffles, lotteries, and sweepstakes. Prizes and awards such as shares of stock, building lots, merchandise, and vacation trips are taxable. The fair market value of the trips, service, or merchandise received is the amount to be included as taxable income. This is also applicable if the recipient disposes of any such item by gift or otherwise."

Q. How can I determine what tax—if any—is due on a vacation prize, which actually cost me money to take?

A. For advice on any specific Federal income tax problem, you should communicate with the Internal Revenue Service office for your district. Only an official ruling can show you the proper procedure to follow in reporting any particular kind of prize contest winnings. An excellent book of general information on this subject is Taxation of Prizes, Awards and Scholarships, by Joseph Arkin, available at $2.00 a copy from Contest Magazine, Upland, Indiana. Mr. Arkin, a Certified Public Accountant, also writes a monthly column for Contest Magazine

called "Paying Taxes on Prizes," which contains much valuable
and interesting material on this important topic.

Q. Is the average commercial contest completely fair and
honest?

A. All contests conducted <u>through the mail</u>—which would
include every one involving any form of written entry—must
conform to Post Office regulations which govern their judging
standards and procedure. That's the best insurance of their
integrity. Even aside from this official controlling factor, no
commercial firm would risk its reputation by sponsoring any
questionable form of promotion. Contests <u>must</u> be fair and honest to serve their prime purpose of benefiting the sponsor's
business.

Q. Are there any continuous contests, open for entries at
any time?

Q. If a contest may be considered as an offer of payment
for usable written material of a specific nature submitted by
anybody, the answer is "Yes." You will find such continuous
cash offers in every issue of <u>The Reader's Digest</u>, <u>Pageant</u>,
<u>True</u>, <u>Cavalier</u>, <u>Playboy</u>, <u>True Story</u>, <u>Family Circle</u>, <u>Woman's
Day</u>, and many other popular magazines. Most of these offers
are made for jokes, quips, anecdotes, or household hints, with
payment ranging from $5.00 to $100, for each acceptable item.
While no national commercial contest is run continuously, the
same sort of competition may be conducted annually—like the
race horse naming contest sponsored every spring by Kentucky
Club. Another annual contest appears in the St. Joseph Calen-
dar distributed free at the start of each year by drug stores
carrying products made by Plough, Inc.

Q. When it is announced that a contest will close on a certain date, does it mean entries must be received by that time
or postmarked not later than the given date?

A. If rules are not clear on the point, always <u>play safe</u> and
consider them to mean that your entries should be <u>received</u>
by the date mentioned—which, in turn, means mailing
them a few days before the deadline.

Q. Are the courses offered by contest correspondence schools worth what they charge?

A. It all depends on your ability to apply their teachings, which have been proven sound and effective in countless contests. According to advertisements, the aggregate winnings of their students amount to nearly ten million dollars. To determine the potential value of their courses for yourself, write for free details to the directors of these contest schools:

Charles A. Kraatz, All-American School, 1429 Spruce Street, Philadelphia 2, Pa.

Wilmer S. Shepherd, Jr., Shepherd School, 1015 Chestnut Street, Philadelphia 7, Pa.

Q. I live on a farm a long way from any city having a contest club; yet I'd like to keep in touch with other contesters. Is there any way I can do so?

A. Yes—through a series of Round Robin letters conducted for contest fans by Mrs. Gladdie Burger, 2820 North Venice Avenue, Tucson, Arizona. Send her a stamped, self-addressed envelope for further information on this correspondence contest club; or see her monthly column, "Robin Round-Up," in Contest Magazine.

Q. Is it possible to make a living entirely from prize winning, by entering every contest in a businesslike way?

A. Absolutely not! It would be the height of folly to expect any such result. Contesting is a hobby, not a job. Whatever prizes come your way are only a welcome supplement to your own or your family's usual source of support, generally providing more pleasure than profit. True, you may win a wad of cash equal to several years' normal earnings—or a car, home or vacation that you couldn't afford otherwise. But you cannot count on that possibility as a substitute for a steady salary or regular income.

Q. What were the largest and smallest prizes ever awarded in any kind of contests?

A. For solving a long series of puzzles and answering 720 difficult questions, Mrs. Lelia Boroughs of Beverly Hills, Calif.,

won $375,000—the biggest prize reported so far. The smallest
award of any specific value on record was a half-cent U.S.
postage stamp given by this writer to Mrs. R. C. Chamberlain
of Chicago for her last line to this limerick:

> Don't scoff at a prize if it's small,
> For it's better than nothing at all.
>   And even a stamp
>   May make you a champ . . .
>
> By gum, you'll lick Franklin—so scrawl!

Q.   From reading winning entries, I know that punning helps
land a prize, especially in limerick and title contests. Since
I'm not very good at this trick, could you tell me if there is
any sure-fire method for composing a pun on any subject?

A.   Yes, you can easily learn how to compose a pun on any
subject but the King—since the King isn't a subject. And there's
a pun for you! Really, though, it isn't at all difficult. Just take
any popular phrase or expression and change it slightly in
sound or spelling. Consider the oft-heard remark, "Long time
no see." A sailor on shore duty might comment: "Long time no
SEA." A low-voiced singer could say: "Long time no C." A
senorita who refuses her Latin lover might make him observe:
"Long time no SI." And when your TV set breaks down in the
middle of your favorite show, you might crack: "WRONG time
no see!" Get the idea? And remember Ed Wynn's classic
switch: "A bun is the lowest form of wheat."

Authoritative Advice

As a special service to readers of this book, the author will
personally answer—to the best of his knowledge and ability—any
reasonable question concerning creative contests in particular
or the contest hobby in general. For a prompt reply, please enclose a self-addressed, stamped envelope or postal card. Send
your queries directly to the author, addressed:

> ALLEN B. GLASSER
> 241 Dahill Road
> Brooklyn 18, New York

GLOSSARY OF CONTEST TERMS

ACROSTIC—formation of a product's or sponsor's name by special arrangement of words in an entry. Generally, the first letter of each line, reading from top to bottom, will make up the name or other message.

ALLITERATION—use of the same starting sound in several words in one group.

ANALOGY—adaptation of words from a particular field (such as sports, music, transportation) to express an entry more effectively.

APTNESS—close adherence of an entry to the specific subject of a contest.

BALANCED PHRASE—an expression that weighs one product virtue against another, as: "Maximum worth at minimum price."

CAPTION—a phrase or sentence describing a picture or cartoon; or a remark attributed to a character therein.

COINED WORD—an artificial word or name, either wholly invented or formed by combination or alteration of ordinary words.

CONTESTANT—one who enters any competition; a contest entrant.

CONTESTER—one who makes a hobby of entering contests; a regular prize seeker.

COUPLET—a complete verse or stanza of two rhyming lines.

CREATIVE CONTEST—a competition based on skillful composition of written entries, not including puzzles.

DEADLINE—the closing date of any contest, for mailing or receipt of entries.

DECORATION—addition of special effects, such as art work, color, picture paste-ups or other embellishment, to an entry.

DEVICE—a contrived expression or deliberate arrangement of words to give an entry an impressive effect.

ENTRANT—anyone who submits an entry in a contest.

ENTRY—a composition submitted to a contest in compliance with its rules.

ENTRY BLANK—an official form which may be required for participation in a contest.

FACSIMILE—a copy of a qualifier (which see) as specified by contest rules.

FOLLOW THROUGH—natural continuity between a contest's starting phrase or given jingle lines and the entry itself.

FORMULA—a device which may be adapted for repeated use in different contests.

GIVE-AWAY—any prize distributed by chance, through lucky drawings or random picking of winners' names from general sources.

HOMONYM—a word pronounced exactly like another, though spelled differently, like "right" and "write."

INNER RHYME—a device using two or more rhyming words within the same line.

JINGLE—any short verse, usually consisting of four lines, of which at least two must rhyme.

JUDGE—(noun) an evaluator of entries who decides upon their relative merit and final standing; (verb) to grade entries according to certain standards.

KEYING—using variations of one's name to identify which of several entries may prove to be a winner.

LAST LINE—the line to be added to an incomplete limerick or jingle.

LIMERICK—a verse of five lines, in which the first, second and fifth lines rhyme with one another, while the third and fourth lines rhyme with each other.

LOCAL CONTEST—a competition open only to residents of the community in which it is held.

METER—the regular rhythm or cadence of a line of verse.

NATIONAL CONTEST—a competition open to all or most of the fifty States.

ORIGINALITY—freshness or novelty of thought and expression—an important factor in evaluating entries.

PARODY—a modified version of a well-known expression, saying, title, proverb or any famous utterance. In contest terminology, "parody" and "paraphrase" are used interchangeably.

PATTERN—same as "formula."

PERSONFICATION—attributing human, sentient qualities, emotions, and actions to inanimate objects.

PROSE—speech or writing that is not deliberately rhymed or rhythmic.

PUN—(as a noun) a word altered for humorous or double-meaning effect; (as a verb) to make a pun.

QUALIFIER—the proof-of-purchase required with an entry, such as a box top, label, wrapper, sales receipt, etc.

QUALIFY—to validate an entry for judging consideration by accompanying it with whatever proof-of-purchase may be required.

QUATRAIN—a verse of four lines, in any rhyming order.

REGIONAL CONTEST—a competition limited to residents of a designated geographical area.

RHYME—corresponding sound between words or syllables.

RHYMING DICTIONARY—a volume of words grouped according to matching terminal sounds or rhymes.

RHYTHM—regular recurrence of accented words or syllables in a line of verse.

SALES POINT—a special virtue of a product emphasized in an entry.

SLANT—(noun) planned inclination of entries to meet stated judging standards; (verb) to strive for that effect.

SLOGAN—a brief, pithy phrase describing the salient feature of some product, or urging a specific course of action.

SPONSOR—(noun) the financial backer of a contest; (verb) to provide funds for the conduct of a contest.

STANZA—a part or division of a poem, comparable to a paragraph in prose.

STATEMENT—the conclusion, in not more than 50 words, of a contest's starting phrase. A longer entry is generally called a "letter."

SWEEPSTAKES—a drawing of winners' names by pure luck or chance, in which skill plays no part.

SYNONYM—a word similar in meaning to another one.

TITLE—same as "caption," though applicable to a wider range of subjects than pictures and cartoons.

TRIAD—a device using three related items or phrases in one entry.

UNIQUENESS—the element of difference in an entry that makes it impossible of duplication by any other submission.

VERSE—a composition in rhymed and/or rhythmical form.

WINNERS LIST—an announcement released by the sponsor upon conclusion of a contest naming all prize winners.

WORD PLAY—contrived arrangement or alteration of words to make an entry more effective.

ZERO—rating of an entry that fails to follow most of the tips given in this book.

INDEX